IDEAS FOR SPELLING

IDEAS FOR SPELLING

FAYE BOLTON & DIANE SNOWBALL

HEINEMANN
Portsmouth, NH

The authors would like to thank the Principal and staff of
Deer Park North Primary School for their co-operation in
the preparation of photographic material for this book.

Heinemann
a division of Reed Elsevier Inc.
361 Hanover Street   Portsmouth, NH03801-3912
Offices and agents throughout the world

ISBN 0-435-08801-7

Library of Congress Cataloguing-in-Publication Data.

Bolton, Faye.
    Ideas for spelling/Faye Bolton & Diane Snowball.
       p.   cm.
    Previously published as: Springboards.
    ISBN 0-435-08801-7
    1. English language – Orthography and spelling – Study and
teaching. 2. Language arts. I. Snowball, Diane.
II. Title. III. Title: Springboards.
LB1574.B62 1993
372.6'32—dc20   93-2542
                                           CIP

First published in the USA in 1993 by Heinemann.
Reprinted 1994.

First published in Australia in 1985 by

Thomas Nelson Australia
102 Dodds Street
South Melbourne 3205

Cover design by Erika Budiman
In-text photographs by David Corke
Typeset in Times by Bookset Pty Ltd
Printed in Australia by
Impact Printing (Vic.) Pty Ltd.

Contents

Introduction

Over the last twenty years a great deal of research has been conducted in a wide range of areas related to spelling — from methods of teaching spelling to children's natural development in spelling ability. Simultaneously, greater understanding about the nature of the English orthography has been acquired.

We have endeavoured to draw together this accumulated knowledge and to present it in such a way that teachers may reflect upon many current practices used in the teaching of spelling and be better equipped to guide children's spelling development.

Considering that it is a desirable educational aim that children become competent spellers, teachers need to know and use the most effective strategies for teaching spelling.

Writing provides the purpose for spelling; consequently a spelling programme should grow out of a significant and active writing programme. Children need to know how to spell words they want to use in their writing. Traditionally, schools have taught spelling from published word lists which may contain either words irrelevant to the children's writing or words that individuals already know how to spell. Current knowledge indicates that it is more effective to view every writing session as a spelling workshop.

Although spelling must be taught according to individual needs in writing, it is also necessary to involve children in a wider programme which purposely exposes them to the various features of the English orthography (written language).

Through the suggestions in this book and the companion programme 'Spelling in Context', teachers will be able to implement a balanced spelling programme within the context of a total language programme so that students become both independent in and confident about their spelling ability.

Faye Bolton and Diane Snowball

1
The context of spelling

Spelling should be viewed in the context of writing rather than as an isolated skill.

What is spelling?

Spelling is a highly complex task that is gradually mastered over a period of time as an individual becomes acquainted with the properties and purposes of written language. It is not merely the memorisation of words. Spelling involves the use of strategies which may vary according to the words being attempted and the knowledge that the writer has acquired through experiences with words.

The social context of spelling

Accurate spelling is highly valued by society. This is understandable, as conventional spelling does facilitate written communication. If children are denied an opportunity to learn conventional spelling, they could be greatly disadvantaged.

Many poor spellers have low self-esteem in relation to their writing ability. This is reinforced by society's tendency to draw subjective conclusions about writers' general attributes if their written work is not word perfect.

Society does have misconceptions about spelling, however. The most outstanding of these is the notion that a good speller is one who spells all words correctly all of the time, and that correct spelling should be attained in the very early years of primary school. Writers who spell all words correctly may in fact only be using words they feel safe with, and may not have any idea how to attempt unknown words.

Invented spelling

In a literate society, most children begin school with some knowledge of the complexities of written language. Many may already have attempted some form of written communication. This should be accepted, acknowledged and nurtured.

Learning to write, like learning to talk, is a developmental process. When learning to talk, children are doing so for a purpose. Because their approximations are accepted and encouraged, they confidently explore the rules governing oral language. By allowing children to explore written language, we allow them to discover its purposes and feel confident about attempting to write words they may not know how to spell. Through this exploration, children acquire knowledge about the nature of the orthography (or written language) and naturally assume a greater responsibility for their own writing. Children who are allowed to experiment, and whose questions about words and spelling are answered, will begin to formulate and later refine ideas about spelling in the same way as they formulated and refined their spoken language.

Children's invented spellings are the learners' attempts to find pattern and order in the spelling system. It is important that writers of all ages are afforded the same conditions for learning to spell as those offered to beginning writers. By being allowed to continue to take risks when attempting unknown words, writers will gradually move towards conventional spelling as they further explore the relationships between the oral and written language. Some invented spellings are more advanced than others (that is, they more closely resemble conventional spellings). By observing such approximations, insights may be gained into what the writer knows and doesn't know about spelling. This in turn provides guidelines for teaching. If children are not allowed opportunities to attempt spellings of unknown words, it is not possible to teach according to their needs.

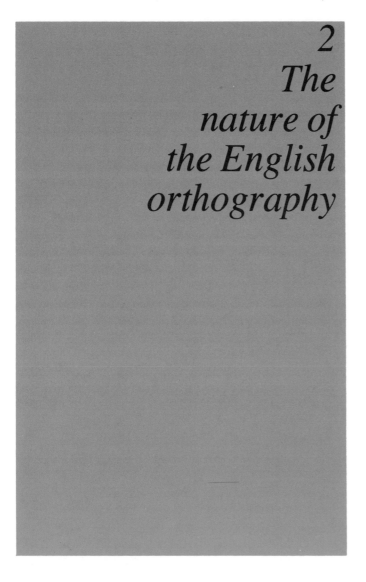

2
The nature of the English orthography

How regular is the English orthography?

Historically, parents and teachers have tended to view the English orthography as merely representing the sounds of the language. From this sound-orientated perspective, it has been concluded that the written language is highly irregular and quite arbitrary. This conclusion has been drawn because many letters can represent more than one sound (e.g. the letter 'o' in 'women', 'oven', 'comb' and 'cot'), and many sounds can be represented by a variety of letters (e.g. the /f/ sound in 'enough', 'off', 'fox' and 'photo').

However, any one sound in the English language can only be represented by a particular set of symbols or graphemes, and any one grapheme can only represent a particular set of sounds.

Furthermore, recent investigations into the nature of the English orthography have focussed on the units of meaning within words. When viewed in this way, the English orthography has emerged as being highly consistent and, in fact, near optimal. Noam Chomsky (1968) argues that English spelling is not an adequate system for representing sounds but, rather, a highly efficient system for representing meanings. Because the orthography represents meaning, and not merely sound, the reader is helped to go straight to meaning. This could provide difficulties for the speller, particularly one who has been taught to rely on a phoneme-grapheme strategy. The efficient speller, however, takes advantage of the structure by using a spelling strategy that takes meaning into account; that is, a morphemic strategy (Chomsky 1970).

In order to help children to learn to spell, the English orthography needs to be investigated according to morphemic relationships, the range of phoneme-grapheme relationships, and the semantic and syntactic influences upon the words.

Morphemic relationships

Morphology is the study of the smallest meaningful units of language. These units are called *morphemes* and may stand alone or be combined with one or more other morphemes to form new words.

Morpheme study is a powerful way to gain an insight into the word-building properties of the English orthography, which in turn facilitates competency in spelling. For example:

1 The word 'unfamiliar' is made up of two morphemes (un + familiar). Recognising the meaning of the prefix 'un' and being able to spell that prefix will assist in the spelling of other words with the same prefix:

   un + desirable = undesirable

   un + natural = unnatural

   un + necessary = unnecessary.

This particularly assists the spelling of words where there may be doubt as to whether the words are spelt with 'n' or 'nn'.

2 The word 'commitment' is made up of two morphemes (commit + ment). Recognising the meaning of the suffix 'ment' and being able to spell that suffix will assist in the spelling of other words with the same suffix:

   advertise + **ment** = advertisement

   entertain + **ment** = entertainment.

3 The word 'someone' is made up of two morphemes (some + one). Recognising that this word is composed of two morphemes, which may already be known, will ensure that the compound word is spelt correctly. The morphemes within the word may also be used as a basis for spelling other related words:

   some + body = somebody

   some + where = somewhere

   any + **one** = anyone

   no + **one** = no one.

In the same way, meaning relationships between other words may be identified. For example:

1 verb tenses:

   play, playing, played

   hop, hopping, hopped

2 plural forms:

>   boy, boys
>
>   church, churches
>
>   brush, brushes
>
>   gully, gullies

3 comparative and superlative forms:

>   green, greener, greenest
>
>   thin, thinner, thinnest
>
>   pretty, prettier, prettiest

4 derivatives:

>   tele/television, telescope, telegraph.

Note that in many instances the use of morphology assists the spelling of a word much more than pronunciation does. Consider the following words in which pronunciation may change from one word to the other, but in which the basic spelling patterns remain constant due to the morphemic relationships:

>   magic, magician
>
>   opposed, opposition
>
>   industry, industrial
>
>   native, nation
>
>   grade, gradual
>
>   mean, meant.

This is particularly useful in words with a silent letter like:

>   sign (signal)   soften (soft).

It is particularly important for the teacher of spelling to be aware of these morphemic relationships between words so that they may be highlighted as important strategies to use when attempting to spell an unknown word.

At the beginning stages of spelling development, children do not have a conscious understanding of the morphological aspects of the English orthography. Initially they use the most obvious aid for the spelling of words; that is, the relationships between sounds and letters.

Phoneme-grapheme relationships

The English orthography uses an alphabet of only twenty-six letters (graphemes) while there are forty-four distinctive sounds (phonemes) in English oral language. To inform children that a letter has only one sound is incorrect; the sound associated with a particular letter is dependent upon the word in which it occurs (see Appendix 5). Letter names are constant, while letter-sound relationships are a limited set of options.

Children should be taught letter names prior to the introduction of phoneme-grapheme relationships so that they have a consistent label for each letter. When teaching phoneme-grapheme relationships, it is important to deal with them in such a way that children do not develop misconceptions.

For instance, if asking children to nominate words which

contain a particular sound, all words containing the target sound, regardless of letter representation, must be accepted. For example:

the sound /ee/ in the following words:

money, receive, leave, see, happy, he, quay, people, amoeba, relieve.

Furthermore, when highlighting a spelling pattern, all words containing such a pattern, regardless of the sound, should be dealt with. For example:

the 'ea' pattern in the following words:

ready, great, leaf.

When spelling a word, the sound-symbol relationship provides great assistance as an initial attack upon the task. This is particularly so for beginning spellers. However, children will gradually realise that merely using this strategy will not always produce correct spelling. For example, the following words would be misspelt if only the sounds in the words were considered:

soften, write, comb, knitting, gnat.

Within the phoneme-grapheme relationship, certain constraints exist:

LETTER PATTERNS

As an example, the word 'mip' could exist in English orthography as it follows the same pattern as words such as 'hip', 'sip', 'tip', 'lip', 'pip', 'rip' and 'zip'. However, a word such as 'ctp' would not occur because it does not follow a conventional pattern. The English orthography predictably has at least one vowel in every word in order to make letter strings pronounceable. Similarly, you would expect to find patterns such as 'ear', 'tion', 'orn', 'ame', 'ough' and 'dge' but not patterns such as 'ij', 'inb', 'amd' and 'iul'.

LETTER SEQUENCES

The letter 's' in the initial position in a word could only be followed by a vowel or the consonants 'c', 'h', 'k', 'l', 'm', 'n', 'p', 'qu', 't', 'w'. Consequently 'sdim' would not be a word in the English orthography but 'swip' could be.

This is probably due to articulation limitations, as some sound sequences are difficult to produce.

POSITIONS OF LETTERS

Although a phoneme may be represented by a variety of graphemes, the position in which it occurs in a word will often influence the choice of grapheme. The phoneme /f/, for example, may be represented by the letters 'f', 'ff', 'ph', and 'gh'. However, if the sound is at the beginning of the word it will only be represented by 'f' or 'ph', but if it is at the end of the word it is not likely to be represented by 'f':

fox, far, frog, photo, Philip, phantom, pharmacy, phase, pheasant, phonology, graph, off, laugh, stiff, puff, rough, tough.

Semantics and syntax

Semantics is the meaning derived from text, according to the experiences that the reader brings to the text. The *syntax* of a language is the order in which words are put together to express meaning.

Because both syntax and semantics add to the meaning of a word they play an integral role in spelling:

Over |**there** is |**their** house.
     |**their** | **there**

This is wonderful|**weather** for ducks.
                 |**wether**
                 |**whether**

Sometimes the total context beyond the sentence is required to determine word meaning:

There is the|**sun.**
            |**son.**

In order to determine the spelling it is necessary to consider the total context in which the sentence is embedded:

There is the **sun**. It is very bright.

There is the **son**. He looks like his father.

Implications for teaching

The teaching of spelling should be based on the nature of the English orthography. Although beginning spellers will rely heavily on phonetic strategies, children should be encouraged as soon as possible to be aware of the meaning relationships between words and to use such knowledge to attempt spellings.

Because of the regularity of the letter patterns of the orthography, spellers become aware of a visual image of words. It is common practice for competent spellers to write a word several ways to decide which one 'looks right'. This practice should be encouraged when children are able to proof-read their writing. There seems little reason to purposely present children with an incorrect image of words as this could impede their spelling ability. Consequently, it is unwise to present activities such as 'unjumble the letters to make a word' or 'detect which words are spelt incorrectly in a particular passage' (written by someone else, with intentional spelling mistakes). Spelling activities are much more productive if they provide correct models of spelling.

Generalisations

Traditionally, it has become common for teachers to teach children spelling rules. However, these rules cannot be consistently applied, since most rules have exceptions. For example, the rule '**i** before **e** except after **c**' in words with an /ee/ sound (receive, deceit, conceive, etc.) does not apply in the case of the word 'seize'.

It is much more appropriate to form generalisations about

the nature of the English orthography, and these are better if *learned* rather than *taught*. Students should be encouraged to form generalisations through multiple encounters with words that exemplify such generalisations.

A variety of generalisations can be made about the nature of the English orthography, relating to both the phonological and morphological aspects of the language.

PHONOLOGICAL GENERALISATIONS

Phonological generalisations are those which relate to the possible symbols which may represent a particular sound, depending upon its position in a word. For example:

the /k/ sound may be represented in the following ways:

duck, Christmas, picnic, trekked, quay, key, racquet, oblique, like, walk.

By listing words with the /k/ sound and noting the symbols that represent the sound, children could form the generalisation that it is not likely that 'ck' will represent the /k/ sound at the beginning of a word. A further generalisation would be that the /k/ sound is not often represented by the symbol 'kk'.

MORPHOLOGICAL GENERALISATIONS

These generalisations relate to the meaning units of the language. For example:

1 Past tense is normally indicated by the letters 'ed' — like, liked.

2 Present participles are normally indicated by the letters 'ing' — run, running.

3 When adding 'ed' and 'ing':
   - if the word ends in 'e', delete the 'e' before adding 'ed' or 'ing' — hope, hoped, hoping
   - if the word ends in a consonant which is preceded by a short vowel, double the consonant before adding 'ed' or 'ing' — hop, hopped, hopping
   - if the word ends in 'y', change the 'y' to an 'i' before adding 'ed' — study, studied.

4 When forming comparatives and superlatives:
   - if the word ends with a consonant and has a short vowel, double the final consonant before adding the letters 'er' and 'est' — fat, fatter, fattest
   - if the word ends with a 'y', change the 'y' to an 'i' before adding 'er' and 'est' — funny, funnier, funniest.

5 When forming plurals:
   - generally add 's' —boy, boys
   - if the word ends with 'ch' or 'sh', add 'es' — church, churches; brush, brushes
   - if the word ends in 'a', add the letter 'e' — larva, larvae.

All such generalisations should be formed only after children have encountered sufficient examples to allow them to draw conclusions. Such examples should be drawn from meaningful contexts in both reading and writing, with teachers being sufficiently alert to capitalise on the best opportunities for highlighting any one generalisation.

Children's writing and oral language development will provide an indication of the appropriate time to encourage the formation of particular generalisations. For example, the use of 's' to form a plural may be discussed with some five-year-olds, but the means of forming past tense may not be dealt with until a later stage of development.

Once generalisations have been formed, they must be continually reviewed and refined as further examples are encountered. Note that it is not necessary to talk about 'exceptions to the rule', as generalisations are only indications of common spelling features, rather than being hard and fast statements.

Learning to spell involves the writer actively identifying and classifying recurring language patterns, or generalisations, in the written orthography and then applying this knowledge to attempt new spellings.

References

Chomsky, N., 'Phonology and Reading', in Levin, H. & Williams, J. (eds), *Basic Studies in Reading*, Basic Books, New York, 1970.

Chomsky, N. & Halle, M., *The Sound Pattern of English*, Harper and Row, New York, 1968.

3

Strategies used by competent spellers

When writing, competent spellers seem to be able to draw upon a variety of knowledge which reflects their awareness of the patterns and structure of words. This knowledge appears to be applied in a systematic manner and usually involves the use of various strategies, including visual, phonological and morphological strategies. Information about these strategies is acquired not from rote memory but from extensive experience with written language.

Good spellers tend to:

- view spelling as a problem-solving task, thus being prepared to attempt unknown words by making use of prior knowledge to predict the most likely spelling
- have a well-developed language competence through exposure to words
- have an interest in words
- have a 'spelling conscience' and consequently be prepared to proof-read their writing
- have a large number of remembered spellings and can therefore write a large number of words as whole units
- have a learning method or systematic procedure for learning new or difficult words
- be confident about their ability to spell
- be able to make generalisations and deductions readily.

They tend to use the following strategies:

- the knowledge of the morphological structure of words and the consequent relationships between words

- the knowledge of grapho-phonic relationships; that is, the variety of sound/symbol relationships, the probability of letter sequences, the likely position of letters in a word and possible letter patterns
- the ability to use visual memory to determine whether a word looks correct
- the ability to apply a large number of generalisations
- the ability to develop and use mnemonics, or memory aids (a **pie**ce of **pie**)
- the ability to use resources such as other people, word lists and dictionaries for a variety of purposes.

Competent spellers in general also articulate words and have swift, legible handwriting.

It is important for teachers to be aware of the strategies that competent spellers use in order to develop the use of such strategies by all children.

It is also important to remember, however, that competency in spelling must be viewed according to the child's stage of spelling development. Beginning spellers attempt words with less knowledge than they will have as their experience with language increases. A visual strategy is obviously of no use to them if they have never seen the word before, and a morphemic strategy, which makes use of the units of meaning in words, can only be utilised by the speller who is aware of their significance (Thomas 1982). Consequently, beginning spellers rely mainly on the sounds heard in a word, while advanced spellers have a wider range of strategies. These strategies may vary according to the word and previous experiences related to the word. The spelling of the word may be compared with a similar known word, morphemic knowledge may be applied, a visual image may be recalled, generalisations may be applied or a phonetic strategy may be used as a starting point.

Reference

Thomas, V., *Learning to Spell: The Way Children Make Use of Morphemic Information*, Curriculum Services Unit, Education Department of Victoria, Carlton, 1982.

4
Stages of children's spelling development

The spelling process

Learning to spell is a complex task which is accomplished over a period of time as an individual experiences and interacts with written language. It should not be assumed that spelling competency is acquired early in the primary years of school, and in fact for some children may not be fully acquired until the early post-primary years.

The acquisition of spelling ability is a developmental process. Young children constantly search for and organise cues that enable them to make sense of their environment, according to their level of cognitive development.

The writing system is part of that environment and it too needs to be made sense of. Spelling requires cognitive processing of information about spoken and written language and knowledge of their interrelatedness. From information gained, the learner generates hypotheses about the written language. Beginning spellers have limited information to draw upon when writing, so they invent spelling as part of the process to make sense of the orthography. Such invented spellings are mistakes only in terms of adult norms and conventional orthography. In the children's terms, these errors are representations of a developing knowledge of the written orthography.

Through intensive exposure to print and personal experiences with writing, children progress towards correct spelling at their own pace. Their invented spellings differ from conventional spelling in many ways, but what is highly significant is the systematic nature of their spellings and the uniformity of these from child to child. Researchers such as

Read (1971), Beers and Henderson (1977), Gentry (1982) and Beers, Beers and Grant (1977) have found that, as children begin to write, the process for learning to spell develops in clearly defined stages for most children. Gentry (1982) classifies these stages of development into precommunicative spelling, semiphonetic spelling, phonetic spelling, transitional spelling and correct spelling.

Although children's writing development begins from the moment they put pen to paper, the beginning of children's spelling development does not occur until they first begin to use symbols to represent written language.

An example of a child's writing before the use of symbols to represent written language

Precommunicative spelling stage

This is so called because the writing is not readable by others. It may be characterised by the following features:

- There may be random strings of symbols, which may be letters or numbers or invented symbols.
- Symbols may be repeated.
- Letters may be in upper and lower case and used indiscriminantly.

Examples:

Although this initial writing is a purposeful attempt to represent words, it may not follow the left-to-right directionality of English spelling, nor does it indicate any knowledge of letter-sound correspondence.

Semiphonetic spelling stage

Unlike spelling in the previous stage, semiphonetic spelling represents letter-sound correspondence. This spelling may be characterised by the following features:

- Spelling is abbreviated, with only one, two or three letters to represent a word:

  TL (table)   BRZ (birds)   OD (old)

  S (said)   SB (stamp)

- There is evidence of using letters to represent sounds which occur in words:

  TP (type)   BT (bit)

- There is evidence of using letter names to represent sounds:

  AT (eighty)   BOT (boat)   LADE (lady)

This strategy may include the use of an incorrect vowel to represent a particular vowel sound; the selected vowel may have been chosen because its letter-name was closest to the vowel sound in pronunciation:

  PAT (pet)   SET (sit)

- There may be left-to-right arrangement of letters.
- The writing may display word segmentation:

  TD Z MDA (Today is Monday)

Examples:

te ALF and te MzdU Ur
Weg LUPz

The elephant and the monsters are wearing jumpers.

I have a swimming pool.

Phonetic spelling stage

The writing at this stage does not look like standard spelling, though to the trained eye and to the writer it is readable and meaningful.

This spelling may be characterised by the following features:

- There may be a match between letters and *all* essential sounds; letters are assigned without regard for acceptable letter sequence or other conventions of English orthography:

    STIK (stick) TABL (table) SEDRLU (Cinderella).

- There may be consistency in representing particular sounds by specific letters, even though they may not be the correct match:

    KAT (cat) KRUM (crumb)

- Letter name strategies may still be used:

    SED (seed) EVRE (every)

- There may be substitution of incorrect letters with similar pronunciation:

    JAP or JRAP (drape) CHUCK or CHRUCK (truck)

  (Note that if you pronounce 'j' or 'dr' slowly, they sound similar and have the same position of articulation.)

- Nasal consonants may be omitted:

    STAP (stamp) WET (went) SWMIG (swimming)

- An incorrect vowel may be added after a correct vowel or consonant:

    HAIT (hat) DERAP (drape)

  (In this instance the child is slowly pronouncing the word and distinctly hears two syllables.)

- Past tense may be represented in different ways, according to the sounds heard:

    PILD (peeled) HIKT (hiked) TRADID (traded)

- A syllable may be represented by the letter 'r':

    BOXR (boxer)

- Word segmentation and spatial orientation are clearly evident.

Example:

When I was sick I went to the bucket. I was not feeling very well. I had to stay in bed.

The spelling up to this stage may appear strange to adults because they have learned to draw on strategies other than pronunciation. However, it should be clear from the examples provided that the children's invented spellings are not just random attempts at words. Nor are they an indication of poor auditory perception or discrimination; in fact beginning spellers have been described as super phoneticians.

It should also be noted that beginning spellers are using their knowledge of phonetics (how sounds are articulated) and *not* phonics; that is, they attend more closely to the characteristics of English sounds than to conventional letter-sound relationships (Beers and Beers, 1981).

For this reason, it is confusing and frustrating for beginning spellers, who have invented spellings rather than having written words in the conventional form, to be told 'sound it out', as that is what they have already done.

Transitional spelling stage

Writers may operate within the transitional stage for a long period of time (even several years) as they move away from the sole use of the phonetic strategy towards the use of visual and morphemic strategies.

At the beginning of this stage there may not be much evidence of conventional spelling, but as writers progress through this stage, a greater number of words will be known.

The spelling at this stage may be characterised by the following features:

- Vowels appear in every syllable: ELAFUNT

- Nasals appear before consonants: COMBD

- Letter name strategy is converted to a vowel and a consonant:

    ELEVATUR instead of LEVATR.

- A vowel is inserted before the 'r' at the end of a word:

    ELEVATUR instead of LEVATR.

- Common English letter sequences are used:
  YOUNITED

- Vowel digraphs appear often: MAIK, MAYK

- The silent 'e' becomes fixed as an alternative for spelling long vowel sounds: LIKE.
  The use of the silent letter 'e' at the end of a word may be over-generalised: SLEPE.

- Inflectional endings (s, 's, ing, est) are spelt conventionally.

- Morphology and visual patterns are used more frequently:
  SOMEBODY instead of SUMBODY.

- Correct letters may be used but in the incorrect sequence:
  CAOCH (coach)   PAECOCK (peacock)
  The writer at this stage does not always know whether the word 'looks right'. This new visual strategy is not yet consolidated to the point where it may be used consistently.

- Alternate spellings may be used for the same sounds in different words:
  RECEEVE   BLEAD   EIGHTEY

- Learned words, i.e. those correctly spelt, generally appear more often.

Examples:

We wentoutof The Biulding and saw The doki'statue.

We went out of the building and saw the donkey statue.

Dancing leones.

Evry sunday I go dancing leones. I like it very much because on Satarday the 28th of may. My family and I are going to a hall. My sister and I are going to dance. Because we loun how to dance and then the children are in the group only if they know it. We have to ware a black skort and a white teshort. A pear of bobby socks and a pear of happy shose.

Correct spelling stage

At this stage the entire word is spelt correctly in most instances. Knowledge of the English orthographic system is firmly established.

The spelling at this stage may be characterised by the following features:

- The speller has a knowledge of morphological structures including prefixes, suffixes, contractions, compound words and derivatives, and is able to use silent consonants accurately.

- The speller has a knowledge of generalisations and the ability to apply them to new situations; for example, doubling consonants when adding 'ing', 'ed', 'er', or 'est'.

- Word environmental constraints are known such as probable letter sequences and the probable position of a letter or letters in a word. For example, the speller will know that the letters 'ck' will not represent the /k/ sound at the beginning of a word.

- The speller has mastery of uncommon spelling patterns and words with irregular spellings.

- The speller has the ability to recognise when a word doesn't look right and to think of alternative spellings.

- A large body of words is spelt automatically.

Example:

School days

When I was small we had teacher called Mrs Hasty and I called her Mrs Pasty. And in prep we had to find out how to spell words by looking at our spelling words. I couldnt find a ~~won~~ word one day so Mrs Camron told me to ~~s~~ work it out and I couldnt. So I started crying. And at play time I used to fall over on perpose so I could get ~~atenshion~~ atention but it didnt work. My big bully in prep was a girl called Sarah. and she used to ~~throw~~ sand in my eyes and say I am going to get my dad to beat you up and he never did. In grade three I got seperated from my best ~~frea~~ _friend_ and found a new friend called Emma Brown

Development through the stages

It is important to allow children to move through the stages of development at their own pace, and this may vary from child to child.

Change from one spelling stage to the next is more or less gradual; examples of more than one stage may be evident in one piece of writing. Even though children have demonstrated an ability to use more advanced strategies with words they know, they may revert to an earlier strategy when confronted with unfamiliar words.

At all stages of development, writers may have a bank of known words (for example, even children at the precommunicative stage may know how to spell their own names). It is likely that high-frequency words will be those in the bank of known words and these may even be written correctly at the first attempt. However, at the earlier stages of development, children are not likely to apply what they know about spelling high-frequency words to the spelling of low-frequency words.

Also at the earlier stages, children may have no preconception of how the word ought to be spelt, or any expectation that there is a right or wrong way to do it (Chomsky 1979). Sometimes they cannot read back what they have written, particularly a while after the writing is done, but the important thing is that children have had the opportunity to experiment with print.

Implications for teaching

Teachers should be aware of the stages of development and of the characteristics of each stage so that they can analyse the different strategies that children use when writing unknown words. Through this awareness, teachers will have an increased understanding of the logic behind children's spelling and should consequently be aware that errors may be due to the child's development and limited exposure to words, rather than an inability to spell.

Children should be encouraged to write as soon as they show an interest in print, and this encouragement should continue upon entry to school. Once the children get started in writing and feel secure in taking risks with spelling, they can go on to write any message at all. The importance lies not in knowing how to spell certain words, but rather in having the means to write any and all words.

Researchers concerned with the learners' awareness and use of writing conventions contend that if teachers can ignore misspellings and instead encourage and reward creativity, expression and fluency, then children will naturally begin to recognise and use proper spelling, syntax and punctuation through reading and writing practice (Bennett, 1981). It has also been observed that children who are just beginning to come to terms with the conventions of writing must feel confident. This confidence is generally lacking in a classroom where correctness is of primary importance (Hauser, 1982). Such classroom practices are likely to lead children to write only words they know how to spell, which in turn leads to unimaginative prose (Graves, 1978).

This may also give a false indication of the children's spelling development, as they appear to be operating in the 'correct' stage. Correct spelling offers no clues to the children's notions of how English orthography works, or to the strategies they are capable of using to attempt unknown words. Developmental spelling levels may only be determined by observing spelling miscues in a number of pieces of writing.

Teachers should be aware of factors that enable children to progress through stages of spelling acquisition. The way in which oral language is developed has important implications for how children can learn to spell. Children learn to talk by active involvement within a speech environment, where experimentation and approximations are accepted and encouraged. Parents respond with great enthusiasm to the child's tentative efforts, concentrating upon the meaning rather than becoming preoccupied with errors. Parents provide models of whole language, giving positive feedback and not expecting children to instantly speak like adults. These same attitudes and conditions should be applied to children's writing development, spelling being a part of this.

This is not to suggest that spelling competency should be acquired through informal learning only; formal spelling study will also increase spelling consciousness. However, formal study should not be in the form of memorising word lists, but should emanate from purposeful writing and reading experiences.

Accuracy in spelling is a gradual process that is acquired through trial and error, modelling by adults and peers, hypothesis testing and opportunities for practice.

Beginning spellers rely heavily on a phonetic strategy which is not very reliable for spelling the English language, but the manner in which they do this may be viewed as extremely competent. As young children's written experience with language increases, other strategies become available to them.

References

Beers, C. & Beers, J., 'Three Assumptions about Learning to Spell', *Language Arts*, Vol 58, No 5, May 1981.

Beers, C., Beers, J. & Grant, K., 'The Logic Behind Children's Spelling', *The Elementary School Journal*, 77 (January 1977), pp. 238-42.

Beers, J. & Henderson E., 'A Study of Developing Orthographic Concepts Among First-Graders', *Research in the Teaching of English*, 11 (Fall 1977), pp. 133-48.

Bennett, S. G., 'What Everyone Should Know (Has Known but Done Little to Implement) about Evaluating Students' Writing', Arlington, VA: ERIC Document Reproduction Service, 1981.

Chomsky, C., 'Approaching Reading Through Invented Spelling', in L. B. Resnick & P. A. Weaver (eds), *Theory and Practice of Early Reading*, Volume 2, Erlbaum, Hillsdale, New Jersey, 1979.

Gentry, J. R., 'An Analysis of Developmental Spelling in GNYS AT WRK', *The Reading Teacher*, Vol 36, No 2, November 1982, pp. 192-199.

Graves, D. H., 'Balance the Basics: Let Them Write', from a report to the Ford Foundation, New York, 1978.

Hauser, C. M., 'Encouraging Beginning Writers', *Language Arts*, Vol 59 (October 1982), pp. 681-686.

Read, C., 'Preschool Children's Knowledge of English Phonology', *Harvard Educational Review*, 41 (February, 1971), pp. 1-34.

5
Activities related to stages of development

The teaching of spelling strategies should not occur until children have reached the transitional stage. However, there are aspects of the English orthography which may be highlighted before they reach this stage.

Although children's writing is an indication of the stage of spelling achievement they have reached and provides insight into each individual's spelling needs, a balanced spelling programme includes activities which help children's spelling achievement to progress. Teachers need to provide opportunities for children to learn more than they already know.

The following activities have been organised according to stages of spelling development and different emphasis has been given to the types of activities more relevant to each particular stage. The activities are suitable for the class or for groups.

Precommunicative spelling stage

PERSONAL WRITING

Allow children to write for themselves daily, from the time they begin preschool and school. Display their writing and accept it as it is. Ask children to read their writing so that they are aware of an audience. (You may wish to record their words on the back of the writing, for your own information.)

SOUND/SYMBOL RELATIONSHIPS

Give the children practice in auditory discrimination.

1 Have the children listen for particular sounds in the initial and final positions. For example:
- What sound can you hear at the beginning of these words: snake, sausage, sun?
- Clap when you hear the /b/ sound at the beginning of a word: cap, bad, tomato, ball.
- Which words have /d/ at the end: bad, yellow, mad, jump?

2 Involve the children in rhyming activities:
- Listen for words which rhyme: bad, run, mad, dad, pop.
- Listen for rhyming words in a poem or rhyme.
- Ask children to suggest words which rhyme with a particular word: 'take' — make, cake, ache, break, brake.

3 Help children to recognise the repeated sound in alliteration:

Peter Piper picked a peck of pickled peppers . . .

4 Provide a correct model of pronunciation and encourage children to articulate words. Observe children who seem to be having speech problems, but remember that it may be developmental. If necessary, seek specialist assistance.

WORD LISTS AND DICTIONARY SKILLS

1 Teach names of the letters of the alphabet using alphabet rhymes and jingles, alphabet books, blocks, charts and friezes. Help children to recognise the 'look' of the letters through activities and games such as letter matching, sorting, tracing and finding a particular letter from a group of letters. Children should also be encouraged to locate letters at the beginning of words; for example, their names, days of the week. Do not be concerned about presenting children with a variety of print styles as children have no difficulty in recognising individual letters in a number of typefaces.

'Young readers are able to get used to a variety of type faces. They find it no more difficult to identify 't' than '✝' or even 'T'. Once children are told to discover that these shapes all represent the one letter they quickly become familiar with them and perceive them without difficulty as the same letter' (Ryan, 1984).

2 Use direct experiences and reading activities to begin the development of class word lists of high interest and high frequency words. Illustrate these when possible.

MODELLING WRITING

Model writing for children in a variety of ways:

- class wall stories

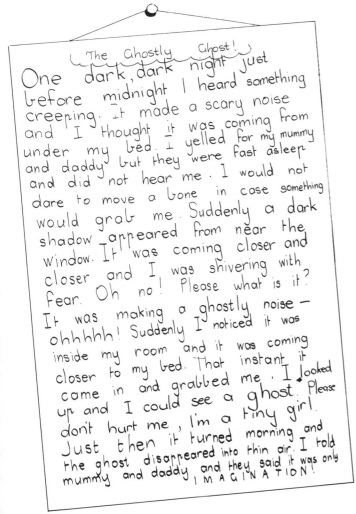

The Ghostly Ghost!

One dark, dark night just before midnight I heard something creeping. It made a scary noise and I thought it was coming from under my bed. I yelled for my mummy and daddy but they were fast asleep and did not hear me. I would not dare to move a bone in case something would grab me. Suddenly a dark shadow appeared from near the window. It was coming closer and closer and I was shivering with fear. Oh no! Please what is it? It was making a ghostly noise — ohhhhh! Suddenly I noticed it was inside my room and it was coming closer to my bed. That instant it came in and grabbed me. I looked up and I could see a ghost. Please don't hurt me, I'm a tiny girl. Just then it turned morning and the ghost disappeared into thin air. I told mummy and daddy and they said it was only IMAGINATION!

What we will do to make our 'magic beans'
1. Water them once a day.
2. Plant them in soil.
3. Plant the seeds under the soil.
4. Watch them every day.
5. Put them next to the window where it is sunny.
6. Take care of the seeds if we want them to grow.

Our beans

On September 12th we planted some beans in a plastic bottle. We put them in soil and we watered them.

September 24th Eleven childrens plants have started to grow. Simons beans are 5 cm tall. We have to take good care of them and water them once a week.

October 1st All of the childrens bean have started to grow because we looked after them. Vicki's plant was 20 tall and it was the biggest. We have to throw the beans in the water out because they smelt horrible. The beans with the cover on it are growing only on one side because the sun is getting to the hole on that. The beans in the sand are growing slower than the beans in the soil.

October 8th All of our childrens plants have grown bigger. Suzies is the biggest and it is 46½ cm tall. We have to take our plants home because the roots will have no room.

October 15th Some of the childrens plants look sick. We will take them home and plant them in our garden so they will have more space for their roots. Suzies plant is the biggest plant was 75 cm.

- class instructions

- thank you letters

Grade 2c,
Westwood P.S.,
Smith St.,
Westwood, 2194.
5th April, 1985

Dear Mr. Lawrence,
     Thank you very much for visiting our school with your fire engine. We loved it when you climbed the ladder. We think you are very brave.

     Yours sincerely,
     Grade 2c

- signs and labels

- class rules

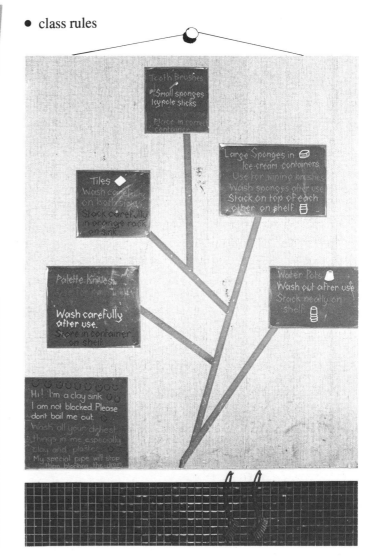

- class diary

Monday, August 8th : The school swimming sports were today. Red house won.

Tuesday, August 9th : Our teacher has a cold because she rescued Timmy yesterday.

Wednesday, August 10th : New boy in our class. He has red hair.

Thursday, August 11th : We had our favourite story in the library

Friday, August 12th : The principal took us for maths and it was too difficult.

- poetry and song charts

- recipes

SOMEONE

Someone came knocking
At my wee small door;
Someone came knocking
I'm sure – sure – sure;
I listened, I opened,
I looked to left and right,

But nought was there
a-stirring
In the still dark night;
Only the busy beetle
Tap-tapping in the wall,
Only from the forest
The screech owls call,
Only the cricket whistling
While the dewdrops fall,
So I know not who came

knocking,
At all, at all, at all.

by Walter de la Mare

Toffee

Ingredients: 2½ cups brown sugar
½ cup water
1 tablespoon butter
2 tablespoons golden syrup
pinch cream of tartar
1 teaspoon vinegar

Method:
1. Collect ingredients
2. Dissolve sugar in water, heating gently.
3. Add butter, syrup, cream of tartar and vinegar.
4. Boil without stirring until a drop sets in cold water.
5. Pour into patty papers.

Makes 24.

- class experience books

- sentence strips

Once upon a time there were three bears.

There was Father bear, Mother bear and

baby bear. One day they went for a walk

into the forest. While they were away, along

When modelling this writing in front of the children, talk about where to start, directionality, use of capital letters and full stops, etc. Help to establish the concepts of words and letters by discussing the number of words in a sentence, and the number of letters in a word.

At this stage you are merely highlighting aspects about written language rather than expecting children to use these in their written work.

Semiphonetic spelling stage

PERSONAL WRITING

Daily writing should continue, with children's work being displayed so that they realise their writing is valued. Attempt to read children's writing and ask them to read it back to you and to other children. The sharing of writing could take place in small groups, and you should encourage children to ask questions about the content of each other's writing. You may wish to record on the reverse side of the paper what the children have written.

Encourage children to invent their own spelling even when they persist in asking how to spell a word. It is vital that children continue to perceive themselves as writers who are willing to take risks with spelling.

At this stage children will perceive that their invented spellings are correct spellings, so there is little point in asking them to proof-read their work. They may have a bank of words that they do know how to spell in the conventional way.

SOUND/SYMBOL RELATIONSHIPS

1 Introduce sound-symbol correspondence through activities such as the following:

- Have children identify and list words with a particular sound, for example:

  words with an /f/ sound:

  fox, off, farm, cough, often, laugh, photo.

  Note that all words with the same sound are accepted, regardless of their spelling patterns. Locate the symbols which represent the sound.

- Ask children to listen for words which begin with a particular sound or end with a particular sound, and to indicate in some way when such a word is said, for example:

  words with a /d/ sound:

  down, bed, desk, bend, said, traded, bad, faded.

  (Intersperse such words with other words which do not contain the sound.)

- Identify and list rhyming words in rhymes and poems. Underline the rhyming parts of each word.

2 Because children at this stage only make use of the phonetic strategy, encourage them to invent spelling according to the sounds they hear in a word:

- 'What do you hear first?'
- 'What do you hear next?'

Encourage clear pronunciation and articulation of words.

WORD LISTS AND DICTIONARY SKILLS

1 Teach children to recognise both upper case and lower case letters, using games, blocks, etc.

2 From examples in children's reading and class writing, select high interest and high frequency words to add to class word lists. Refer to these lists when writing class stories etc.

MODELLING WRITING

1 Continue to model writing in a variety of ways.

2 Establish purposes for writing so that children have ample opportunity to attempt spelling. For example:

- Set up a writing table or area in the classroom with a variety of writing implements and paper.

- Have a class letter-box so that children may write letters to other people.

- Children could write shopping lists when going on an excursion to the supermarket.

- Ask children to write stories after an excursion or other experience.

- Make the children's 'stories' into books, by providing a cover for their piece of writing.

Phonetic spelling stage

PERSONAL WRITING

Children continue to write daily, while the teacher encour-ages children to attempt all spelling. The teacher continues reading children's writing, asking them to read it back and then to other children. Ask questions about the content and allow other children to ask questions as well. In this way children may be more willing to attempt unknown words for which they need to invent spelling.

Children's bank of known words may have increased, and proof-reading habits may be established by expecting children to proof-read their known body of words. They may also be starting to make use of other resources such as class word lists and wall stories to confirm their attempted spellings.

SOUND/SYMBOL RELATIONSHIPS

1 Continue the exploration and indentification of sound/symbol relationships, now with the inclusion of medial sounds, for example:

words with the /ee/ sound:

leave, meat, believe, every, money, people, machine, quay, key, ski.

These words should be selected from children's own writing, from class writing and word lists (in all curriculum areas) and from stories being read. As other words are located with the same sound, these are added to the list.

The words may then be regrouped according to their spelling patterns:

leave	meet	be**lie**ve	bel**ie**ve
leaf	sleep	receive	thieve
meat	feel	delete	thief
cheap	keep	she	
		he	

mon**ey**	rec**ei**ve	prec**e**de	mach**i**ne
honey	deceive	delete	
monkey	receipt	complete	p**eo**ple
donkey			

ever**y**	sk**i**	chass**is**	qua**y**
happy	Ali		
nobody	spaghetti		
any			
many			

2 Identify and list rhyming words from rhymes and poems. Underline the rhyming parts of words and note whether they have the same or different spelling patterns. List other words which rhyme with the listed words:

> Little Jack **Horner**
> Sat in the **corner**
> Eating his Christmas **pie**
> He put in his **thumb**
> And pulled out a **plum**
> And said what a good boy am **I**.

Horner, **corner**, sauna . . .

thumb, **plum**, sum, chum, some, come . . .

pie, **I**, sky, tie, try, buy, by, high . . .

3 Choose a word that children know and substitute letters to form new words. Ask children how one word may be changed to make the next one:

pot	pot	pot
cot	po**p**	p**i**t
dot	po**d**	p**e**t
rot		p**a**t
lot		p**u**t

Note: Do *not* begin with the list of words, but develop the list as children suggest the substitution of one letter.

4 Also build words from a base word:

- by adding a letter. Note that at this stage the words should be those in which purely phonetic strategies may be used:

  an

  and

  hand

  handy

- by deleting a letter:

  chat

  hat

  at

5 Play games such as:

- **Rhyming Ping-Pong**   Play in pairs. The object is to name as many rhyming words as possible within a given time. The player who calls out the last word when the time expires is the winner. For example, the first player says 'play', second player says 'stay', first player says 'hey', second says 'weigh', etc. This game could be played with the entire class, perhaps in relay.

- **Hocus Pocus**   Play in pairs, with children inventing two-word rhyming phrases within a given time; for example, night-flight, fat-cat, golden-holden, great-mate. The player who calls out the last rhyming phrase when the time expires is the winner.

WORD LISTS AND DICTIONARY SKILLS

Continue the development of class lists by incorporating theme and topic words and high frequency words as they arise, and refer to the lists when writing class stories, etc.

Children will realise that it is more difficult to locate particular words as the list becomes larger. They will recognise the need to organise the words for easier location. Encourage the children to suggest ways to regroup the words, one way being according to the initial letter. Write words from the list onto separate cards, enabling the children to regroup them according to their first letter. A chart or a word box may then be developed for each letter of the alphabet. For example:

Aa

apple

ape

aunt

Illustrations or pictures may be placed beside appropriate words to assist word recognition.

Some children may begin to refer to these lists for some words in their own writing, but be sure that children do not think that they have to know how to correctly spell a word before attempting to write it.

Children could begin an individual 'Words I Know How to Spell' card for words which they spell correctly in their writing.

```
 Words  I Know How to Spell       Sue
 and                    have
 family                 here
 school                 birthday
 like                   from
 mum                    any
 teacher                aunt
```

To assist children to learn words that they are interested in, you may also provide them with 'have a go' cards for trying words they are attempting to write. 'Have a go' cards may be organised in a variety of ways. For example:

1st try	2nd try	Correct spelling	Copied spelling
Child attempts spelling		Teacher writes the required word if the child's attempts are not the conventional spelling.	Child copies correct model by using the process: Look at word and say it Cover the word Write the word as a whole unit (not letter by letter) Check spelling. If incorrect, repeat procedure. (Horn, 1919)

Note: Encourage children to look at the word and say the word as a whole, rather than letter by letter or syllable by syllable. When writing the word, the children should not say it letter by letter and should not check the word until the whole word has been written.

'The brain does not decide to write one letter at a time, but rather whole groups of letters, often entire words, which it produces as integrated movement sequences. It is these integrated movement sequences — muscle memories, so to speak — that provide a completely independent alternative resource for remembering how to write words correctly' (Smith, 1982).

This strategy is introduced at this stage to encourage appropriate spelling habits, even though children may not yet know whether or not their attempts look right for many words. This is a valuable record of children's knowledge about spelling.

Known words may then be added to the 'Words I Know How to Spell' card.

Introduce simple published picture dictionaries so that children become aware of this type of resource. Children could browse through them as they develop an interest in words and may refer to them to confirm an attempted spelling.

Ensure that children are aware of the sequence of letters in the alphabet. Play games to increase this awareness:

- Which letter comes after 'd'?
- Which letter comes between 'l' and 'n'?

MODELLING WRITING

Continue to model writing in a variety of ways (see pages 24 to 28) and ensure that children have access to a wide range of reading materials on many topics, so that they are exposed to a large bank of different words.

Transitional spelling stage

PERSONAL WRITING

Continue to write daily, encouraging children to attempt all spelling. Ask children to read their writing and attempt to proof-read known words. If writing is to be published, spelling should be corrected. Encourage the use of class word lists, wall stories, and other resources to confirm their attempted spellings.

SOUND/SYMBOL RELATIONSHIPS

Continue the exploration and identification of sound-symbol relationships and note visual patterns within words.

1 Identify words with a particular sound and classify them into spelling patterns. Deduce generalisations about the probability of particular patterns occurring in the various positions within a morpheme or word. For example:

the sound /k/ in:

duck, picnic, bionic, atomic, cat, cholera, Christmas, kitten, luck, cholesterol, cattle, kangaroo, unique, technique, talk, quay, lucky, queue, antique, trekked, kite, walk, hulk, make, take, quack, chalk, ache.

du**ck**	pi**c**ni**c**	**ch**olera	**k**itten
quack	cat	Christmas	kite
luck	cattle	cholesterol	hulk
lucky	bionic	ache	make
	atomic	technique	take
			kangaroo

ta**lk**	uni**que**	tre**kk**ed
walk	technique	
chalk	antique	
	queue	
	quack	
	quay	

The following generalisations can be made:

- that 'ck' does not appear at the beginning of a word and is mostly at the end of a morpheme
- that 'ch' appears more frequently at the beginning of a word
- that 'c' does not usually appear at the end of a word unless it is part of 'ic'.

These generalisations should be reviewed and refined as other words are added to the list.

2 Identify and list words with the same spelling pattern even though they may be pronounced differently; that is, make use of the visual strategy. For example:

words with 'oo' spelling pattern:

look, blood, loose, loosen, flood, book, tool, hood, mood, stoop, brood.

Regroup them according to sound patterns:

look	blood	loose
book	flood	loosen
hood		mood
		stoop
		brood

An example of an activity devised to focus attention upon a particular letter, letter combination or visual pattern is shown below. Delete the pattern being 'spotlighted', as in the following words containing the pattern 'ei':

n _ _ ghbour

h _ _ fer

_ _ ght

l _ _ sure

rec _ _ ve

The children rewrite the entire words, filling in the missing letters.

3 Use base words to form new words by substituting, adding or deleting letters:

tot	at	us	am
shot	mat	bus	ham
shop	mate	bush	sham
slop		bushy	shame
slope			same
			Sam
			am

4 Use the letters of a word to form new words and regroup the new words according to both spelling patterns and sound patterns:

Hippopotamus: spot, pot, hot, hip, am, Pam, must, post, shot, ham, stamp, pat, tap, host, top, put, past, taps, tops, spat, spit, shut, hut, Sam, map, maps, sham, mash, mast, huts, oh, hit, pith, push, sip, sap, mop, pip, pop, pup, tips, etc.

Regroup according to spelling patterns:

sp**ot**	h**ip**	**am**	m**ust**	**post**
pot	sip	Pam		host
hot	pip	ham		
shot	tips	stamp		
		Sam		

p**at**	**tap**	p**ast**	t**op**
hat	taps	mast	tops
mat	map		mop
spat	maps		pop
	sap		

Regroup according to sound patterns:

am	past	put	hush	pith	spot	post
Pam	mast		shut	spit	pot	oh
ham			hut	hit	hot	host
stamp			must	hip	shot	
sams			huts	sip	top	
sham			pup	pip	mop	
tap				tips	tops	
taps					pop	
map						
maps						
sap						

Note palindromes; that is, words in which the letters may be reversed, still spelling the same word:

pip, pup, pop.

Also note words which make different words when letters are reversed:

spit/tips, pat/tap, top/pot, taps/spat, map/Pam.

5 Find words within words, without changing the sequences of letters. This helps children note visual patterns within words:

teacher	hearth
tea	he
ache	hear
each	ear
her	earth
he	art
teach	heart

6 Play games in pairs or small groups using a set of letter tiles or cards (with multiples of each letter and more of the most frequently used letters):

- **Letter Cross**   Place all letters face down. Each player selects sixteen letters and makes as many words as possible within a given time:

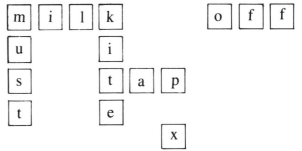

Score one point for each letter used and two points for letters used in more than one word.

- **Build-a-Word**   Place all letters face down. Each player selects eight letters and attempts to make words:

Letters may be replaced from the turned-down tiles and are used to add to words or to make new words:

At the end of the game each player scores one point for every letter used.

- **Letter Mix-up**   Play this the same way as Build-a-Word but players total their score after each turn. Letters may then be rearranged or used with new letters to form new words. If letters can be rearranged, score double points:

7 Play games such as Rhyming Ping-Pong (see page 31) with the teacher listing the words. After the game is played, use the list to discuss alternate spellings according to meaning:

> weigh, way, whey.

WORD LISTS AND DICTIONARY SKILLS

Continue development of class alphabet lists, incorporating theme and topic words as they arise and referring to the alphabet lists when writing class wall stories. Encourage children to refer to these lists when *checking* words in their own writing.

From a class alphabet list on the theme of football

Be sure that these word lists are referred to often to explore the sound-symbol relationships and visual patterns mentioned above.

Children could begin individual alphabet books by transferring the 'Words I Know' into alphabetical grouping. In this way they can easily find words when checking spelling.

Note that the words are listed only according to the letter names they begin with, that is, in twenty-six groups.

Words I Know

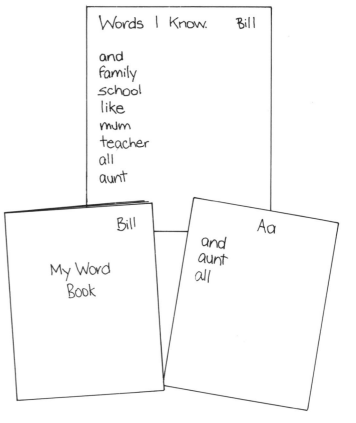

If children enter their own words in their word books check them frequently to ensure that spelling is correct.

Provide a range of resources for children to peruse and refer to for writing; for example, picture dictionaries, dictionaries, word books, topic books, thesauri. Point out to children that published dictionaries are usually organised in alphabetical order. If you have topic word books or thesaurus type dictionaries, compare their organisation with alphabetical dictionaries.

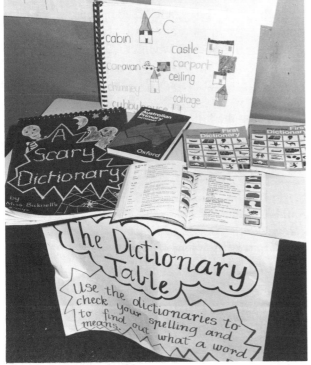

The class dictionary table

Use alphabetical dictionaries and word books to introduce simple location skills for learning how to use such resources. For example:

- Find the page where the 'c' words begin.
- Find the first word in the 'f' list.

Later in the transitional stage, do activities which will increase children's ability to locate information according to alphabetical order.

1 Have children arrange themselves in alphabetical order, using the beginning letters of their first or last names. Ask children what could be done when arranging more than one person with the same initial letter. If necessary, introduce them to the idea of using the second and subsequent letters.

2 Give children opportunities to find information in telephone directories, and make a class telephone directory.

3 Children could use a street directory to locate class members' addresses. Some children may require assistance in mapping skills.

4 Organise category words such as animals, sports, car models, etc. into alphabetical order.

5 Use commercially published books of alphabetical word lists to locate given words, teaching children how to find the appropriate page quickly and the appropriate place on the page. (It is easier for children to learn these skills from such lists rather than from dictionaries with definitions.) After these skills are developed, use simple dictionaries without complex entries for each word.

Continue to provide 'have a go' cards for children, perhaps increasing the number of columns for children's attempts. For many words, the children may still not recognise whether or not their attempts look correct.

Introduce children to the notion of using a memory aid, or *mnemonic*, to remember some words. Such memory aids need to be relevant to the individual and may vary from child to child. For example:

Problem words	Memory aids
there/their	associate 'here' and **there**
were/where	associate 'here' and w**here**
hear/here	associate 'ear' and h**ear**
February	Ask: 'Are you ('**r**' '**u**') having a birthday in Feb**ru**ary?'
dinner (not diner)	I'll have **two** helpings for di**nn**er
quiet/quite	qui**et** as **ET** hiding in the cupboard

A mnemonic chart

MODELLING WRITING

Continue modelling writing in a variety of ways and continue to provide a wide range of reading materials.

MORPHEMIC RELATIONSHIPS

Help develop an awareness of the morphemic or meaning aspects of related words. This should be introduced over a period of time as the children's writing exhibits more correctly spelt words. For example, compound words may be introduced early in the transitional stage, whereas derivatives may be introduced when children are beginning to spell more words correctly. Such morphemic strategies can of course only be introduced when children know the meaning of the words chosen as examples.

When using the following types of activities, begin with words from children's own writing, or from other sources such as stories being read or topic lists in various curriculum areas.

1 Build ongoing lists of word families, beginning with known words. These can depict the use of tenses, plurals, comparatives and superlatives as well as prefixes and suffixes:

> happy, happier, happiest, unhappy, happiness, happily
>
> kick, kicked, kicking, kicks
>
> operate, operating, operated, operator, operation, inoperate, operable, inoperable, operates

entertain, entertainer, entertainment, entertains, entertaining, entertained

opportunity, opportunist, opportunities, inopportune

satisfy, satisfied, satisfies, satisfying, satisfactory, unsatisfactory, satisfaction, dissatisfied, dissatisfaction, satisfactorily

buy, buying, bought, buys, buyer

chemist, chemistry, chemical, alchemist, chemically

care, caring, cared, cares, careful, careless, carefully, carelessly, caringly.

2 Make ongoing lists of comparatives and superlatives and deduce generalisations (e.g. change 'y' to 'i' and double the consonant when the word has a short vowel):

pretty, prettier, prettiest

good, better, best

fat, fatter, fattest

late, later, latest.

3 Make ongoing lists of words and their plurals and deduce generalisations:

sheep, sheep	chief, chiefs
glass, glasses	potato, potatoes
church, churches	antenna, antennae
delivery, deliveries	focus, foci
frog, frogs	child, children
wolf, wolves	box, boxes

die, dice	tooth, teeth
mouse, mice	brush, brushes.
criterion, criteria	

Particularly note that the end sound may be an /s/ or /z/ but the spelling may be the same:

frogs, snakes.

An example of the type of activity related to singular and plural forms is as follows. Children write the singular form of these words. They can then underline each part of the word that differs from the other, for example:

volcano<u>es</u>	volcano
wharves	_____
octopuses	_____
formulae	_____
leaves	_____
children	_____
monkeys	_____
echoes	_____
masses	_____
solos	_____
boxes	_____
teeth	_____

4 Build ongoing lists of occupation words which end in the suffixes 'or' or 'er'. Regroup according to spelling pattern, noting that the end sound is the same:

butcher   operator

miner   doctor

boxer   tailor

greengrocer   surveyor

baker   author

fishmonger

Also list other words which end with 'er' or 'or':

computer   elevator

toaster   refrigerator

paper

typewriter

Form generalisations about the type of word that ends in 'er' and 'or'.

5 Build ongoing lists of verbs and their various tenses and use them to deduce generalisations (e.g. doubling the consonant when the word has a short vowel, deleting 'e' before adding 'ing', etc.):

bubble, bubbling, bubbled

push, pushing, pushed

catch, catching, caught

go, going, gone

put, putting, put

pop, popping, popped

ski, skiing, skied

fly, flying, flew

cry, crying, cried.

Particularly list words ending in 'ed', noting that with three types of pronunciation (walked, pulled, added) the spelling is the same.

6 Build words from parts of compound words:

everyone

everything   no **one**

everybody   some**one**

everywhere   any**one**

grandfather

grandmother   step-**father**

granddaughter   god**father**

grandparents   **father**-in-law

grandson

To assist children to understand the concept of a compound word do word sums such as:

any + body = _____

sun + _____ = sunburn

_____ + coat = raincoat.

Also note that when some compound words are formed, part of one of the component words may be left out:

where + ever   = wherever

all + together = altogether

all + most   = almost

all + ready   = already.

Children should be lead to form generalisations through questions similar to the following:

- What has happened in each of these compound words?
- Does this happen with any other listed compound words?
- Which letters have been dropped? Is this the same each time?

7 Teach meaningful words together, particularly when children have difficulty in spelling:

two : twin, twice, twenty

clothes : cloth

lone : one

foreword : word

aloud : loud

8 Investigate the meaning of well-known derivatives and build up a list of words based on the derivative:

television

telephone

telegram

telescope

telephonist

telepathy

telex

telegraph

telecommunication

Be sure that your classroom has at least one dictionary in which root words may be located. Highlight the meaning link between the words and consequently the same spelling pattern.

Correct spelling stage

PERSONAL WRITING

Continue to write daily and as children are now able to spell most words correctly they should proof-read all written work. If writing is to be published, spelling is to be corrected with children using resources to confirm their spellings.

SOUND/SYMBOL RELATIONSHIPS

Continue the exploration and identification of sound/symbol relationships and note visual patterns within words.

1 Identify words with a particular sound and classify them into spelling patterns. Deduce generalisations about the probability of particular patterns occurring in various positions within a morpheme or word and discuss the meaning of homophones (words that sound the same). For example:

/or/ sound:

saw, sore, caught, awkward, paw, pore, poor, pour, sure, shore, four, for, hawk, fore, tall, corpse, corps, awe, ore, oar, floor, taught, taut, sort, sought,

ought, ball, bald, called, fort, fought, forte, bore, boar, chalk, walk, talk, hoard, horde, stalk, board, bored, fork, cork, pork, stork, balk.

s**aw**	s**ore**	**for**	p**oor**
paw	pore	sort	floor
awe	shore	corpse	
hawk	fore	fort	**corps**
awkward	bore	horde	
	ore	forte	**oar**
w**al**k	bored	fork	boar
talk		stork	hoard
chalk	bald	cork	board
stalk	tall	pork	
balk	called		
	ball		p**our**
c**aught**		s**ought**	four
		ought	
taught	s**ure**	fought	**taut**

The following generalisations can be made:

- It is uncommon for the symbols 'ure' and 'orps' to represent the /or/ sound.
- When the /or/ sound is followed by a 'k', the letters representing the /or/ sound are likely to be 'aw', 'al' or 'or'.

Homophones: Group the homophones, discuss their meanings and begin to develop a homophone chart including illustrations or statements to explain meaning.

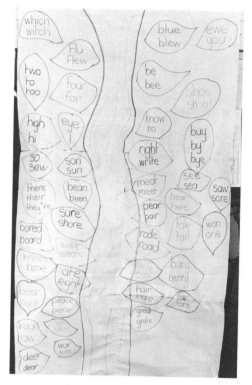

An example of a class homophone chart

Encourage children to refer to resources such as *The Australian Writer's Wordbook* to check homophone meanings. For example:

...saw
(see also *soar, sore*)

...sorcerer

sore
(see also *saw, soar*)

say, says, saying, said...

...soap

soar
(see also *saw, sore*)

sorrow

sorry...

soccer...

As the homophone chart develops, it may be more practical to produce a class homophone dictionary with 'see also' references. For example:

awe (see also 'or', 'oar', 'ore')

He was in **awe** of his hero.

2 Identify and list words with the same spelling pattern even though they may be pronounced differently; that is, make use of the visual strategy. For example:

words with 'ui' spelling pattern:

build, guild, guide, suit, fruit, suite, builder, building, tuition, fruition, guiding, guided, built, guilt, suitable, suitor, suited, suitability, suicide, suicidal, ruin, nuisance.

Regroup according to sound patterns:

build	suit	suite
builder	suitable	
building	suitor	
guild	suitability	
built	suited	tuition
guilt	fruit	

fruition	guide	nuisance
suicide	guided	
suicidal	guiding	
ruin		

3 Note words with silent consonants from children's writing, reading materials and class topic lists. Develop a chart of silent consonants and group according to type:

knee	**g**nu	autum**n**	com**b**
knock	gnash	solemn	tomb
knife	gnat	column	bomb
knit		condemn	limb

sof**t**en	**w**rite	sig**n**	**p**sychology
often	wrong	resign	psychiatrist
nestle	wriggle	design	
wrestle	wrinkle	align	

Form generalisations about letters which are silent at the beginning of a word or the end of a word.

4 Use base words to form new words by substituting, adding or deleting letters. At this stage such an activity should be made more complex by providing the initial and final word, with students devising means of arriving at the final word.

cold ⎯⎯⎯⎯⎯→ warm

cold, cord, card, ward, warm

or cold, cord, word, ward, warm

Children can play in pairs devising such word puzzles for each other.

This can also be played by providing clues for each word in the chain:

boy

b _ y   —   a body of water

ba _   —   to prevent

_ an   —   an adult male

5 Find and write as many words the letters of which may be:
- reversed to form a new word, e.g. top/pot
- reversed to form the same word, e.g. madam
- changed in sequence to form a new word, e.g. dear, dare, read.

6 Find words within words without changing the sequence of letters:

transcribe

ran

an

scribe

crib

rib

be

7 Develop word pyramids by increasing either the number of letters or syllables each time:

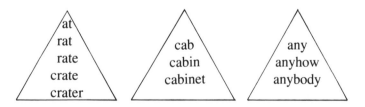

8 Play games such as:
- **Word Rummy**   This can be played in pairs or small groups using a set of consonant cluster cards and a set

of word ending cards; for example:

bl	dr	sc	thr
br	gn	sm	shr
ch	gr	st	squ

and

ad	awl	ing	alk
at	ay	ire	ump
ate	ile	oop	ide

Play a form of card rummy. Deal out five cards to each player and place the other cards face down in a stack. Players use cards in their own hands to form words. For each turn the player draws a card from the stack, forms a word if possible and discards one card. Players have the option of picking up a card from the discard pile rather than drawing from the 'face-down' pile.

- **Endless Chain**   Play this in pairs with one child writing a word and the other child in turn writing a word that begins with the last letter or grapheme of the previous word. The child who has just completed a word at the end of a given time is the winner. This could be increased in difficulty by requiring each child in turn to write a word with one more letter than the previous word. For example:

    pot → talk → kiosk → karate → endless → sandwich → happiness → scholastic, etc.

- **Hangman**   Play Hangman as usual but encourage the children to guess the sequential probability of letters rather than guessing wildly. For example:

    c _ _ _ _

The only letters which could follow the 'c' would be 'a', 'e', 'h', 'i', 'l', 'o', 'r', 'u', 'y' or 'z':

    c **h** _ _ _

The third letter can only be an 'r' or a vowel:

    c h **i** _ _

In order to encourage this logical guessing, play this game as a class before children play it in pairs.

- **Word Blanks**   To encourage the knowledge of sequential probability, provide the first and last letters of a word, with children listing as many words as possible by inserting a given number of letters. For example:

    p _ _ **d**

    paid, pond, prod, plod.

If played in pairs, the one who writes the most words in any given time is the winner.

- **Word Squares**   Provide a card with a letter in each square and children locate as many words as possible horizontally, vertically and diagonally:

p	t	u	n	a	v
c	o	k	e	p	t
r	o	s	o	i	i
z	k	t	n	p	m
t	s	a	e	e	e
g	o	n	e	y	b

- Play commercial games such as Scrabble, and do crossword puzzles.

WORD LISTS AND DICTIONARY SKILLS

Continue to develop dictionary skills by providing a wide range of types of dictionaries. Teach children how to read complex entries in order to confirm spelling. Here is an example from *The Little Macquarie Dictionary*:

de·ceive, *v.*, **-ceived**, **-ceiving. 1.** to mislead by a false appearance or statement. **2.** to be unfaithful to; commit adultery against. – **deceit**, *n.* – **deceitful**, *adj.*

Children need to be taught how to locate the base word in order to locate a related word. For example, to find the spelling of 'deceiving' they need to locate 'deceive'.

Generalisations about morphemic aspects (such as noun endings, adverb endings, comparative and superlative forms, compound words and verb tenses) of words are readily deduced from a dictionary, as the following example from *The Australian Primary Dictionary* shows:

watering-can

watering-can *noun*
a container with a long spout, for watering plants.

waterlogged *adjective*
completely soaked or filled with water.

water-melon *noun*
a large, smooth melon with juicy pink flesh.

water polo *noun*
a game played by swimmers with a ball like a football.

waterproof *adjective*
that keeps water out. *a waterproof coat.*

water-rat *noun*
a large Australian rat with webbed hind feet.

water-ski *noun*
one of a pair of skis of which someone stands for *water-skiing*, skimming over the surface of water while being towed by a motor boat.

watertight *adjective*
1 that water cannot get into. *watertight boots.* **2** that cannot be changed or questioned. *a watertight agreement.*

waterway *noun*
a route that ships can travel on.

waterworks *noun*
the place from which water is supplied to a district.

watery *adjective*
1 of or like water. **2** full of water.

watt *noun*
a unit of electric power.

wattle *noun*
1 acacia. **2** a lobe hanging down from the throat or chin of certain animals and birds. **3 wattle bird,** a honeyeater with red wattles hanging each side of the throat.

wave *verb* (**waved, waving**)
1 to move your hand to and fro, usually to say hello or goodbye to someone. **2** to move to and fro or up and down. **3** to make hair into waves or curls.

wave *noun*
1 a ridge on the surface of water, especially on the sea. **2** a curving piece of hair; a curl. **3** a period or surge of something strong. *a wave of anger.* **4** one of the wave-like movements in which sound, heat, light, etc. travel. **5** the action of waving.

wavelength *noun*
the size of a radio wave or electric wave.

waver *verb*
to be unsteady or uncertain; to move unsteadily.
waverer *noun*

wavy *adjective* (**wavier, waviest**)
full of waves or curves.

wax *noun* (**waxes**)
a slippery substance that melts easily. *Wax is used for making candles, crayons, and polish.*
waxy *adjective*

wax *verb*
to grow bigger.

waxwork *noun*
a model of a person, etc. made of wax.

way *noun*
1 a road or path. **2** a route; the direction or distance to a place. **3** how something is done; a method. **4** a respect. *It's a good idea in some ways.* **5** a condition or state. *Things are in a bad way.* **6 no way,** (*informal*) that is impossible; that is not true.

W.C. short for **water-closet.**

we *pronoun*
a word used by someone to refer to himself and other people who are doing, thinking, etc. the same as himself.

weak *adjective*
not strong; easy to break, bend, defeat, etc.
weakly *adverb*, **weakness** *noun*

weaken *verb*
to make or become weak or weaker.

weakling *noun*
a weak person.

wealth *noun*
1 riches; much money or property. **2** a large quantity. *This book has a wealth of illustrations.*

wealthy *adjective* (**wealthier, wealthiest**)
rich.

weapon *noun*
something used to hurt other people in a battle or fight.

wear *verb* (past tense **wore**; past participle **worn**; present participle **wearing**)
1 to be dressed in something. *I wore that dress last night.* **2** to have something attached to your clothes. *He often wears that badge.* **3** to damage something by rubbing or using it; to become damaged like this. *Your sleeve has worn thin.* **4** to last. *This cloth wears well.* **5** (*informal*) to put up with something. *I'll just have to wear it.* **6 wear off,** to become less; to disappear. **7 wear out,** to make or become weak or useless.
wearer *noun*

wear *noun*
1 clothes. *men's wear.* **2** gradual damage done by rubbing or using something.

weary *adjective* (**wearier, weariest**)
tired.
wearily *adverb*, **weariness** *noun*

weasel *noun*
a small, fierce animal with a slender body.

weather *noun*
1 the rain, snow, wind, sunshine, etc. at a particular time or place. **2 under the weather,** feeling ill or depressed.

weather *verb*
1 to expose something to the rain, sun, etc. *This timber is weathered.* **2** to come through something successfully. *They weathered the storm.*

weatherboard *noun*
1 thin wooden boards nailed so that they overlap and form a protective covering to keep off rain. **2** a building, often a house, constructed in this way.

Also teach children to locate the meanings of roots or prefixes, in both the body of the dictionary and in the appendices:

pre-, *pref.* before (in time, place, order, or importance).

Teach children how to use the most appropriate dictionary for the purpose required, e.g. dictionary of synonyms, antonyms, idioms, colloquialisms, thesaurus, etc. Refer to Appendix 6 for a list of the various dictionaries which either the school library or class libraries should contain.

Children should continue to use 'have a go' cards and to devise memory aids for remembering the spelling of some words:

business: take a **bus in** to your business.

all right: two words like all wrong.

MODELLING WRITING

Continue modelling in a variety of ways and continue to provide a wide range of reading materials.

MORPHEMIC RELATIONSHIPS

Continue to highlight the importance of morphemic strategies for spelling (see pages 38 to 41). Refer to Appendices 2, 3 and 4 for lists of roots, prefixes and suffixes.

Further examples of activities include:

1 Provide lists of words that can be used in various combinations to form compound words. Individually or in pairs, children form as many compound words as possible from two columns like the following:

grand	room
door	man
police	mother
rain	box
mail	bow
bed	ball
snow	drop

Such words could be made into two decks of cards and used in card games such as Fish or Rummy.

Compound words and their opposite compound word could also be listed:

outside, **in**side

nothing, **every**thing

everybody, **no**body

2 Using a root word, form as many words related in meaning as possible, by using the plural form, prefixes, suffixes, changing tenses, etc:

social: anti-social, sociable, socially, socialite, unsociable, society, socialise, socialist

drive: driving, driven, driver, drove, drover, droving, drivable, undrivable, drive-in

port: transport, deport, report, reporter, deportment, reporting, portable, portfolio, portly, important, support, export, import, portage.

3 From children's reading and writing, groups of words may be formed that seem to belong together in meaning. Write such words on cards and have children check definitions in a dictionary, noting the meaning of the root word as well. Write the definitions on the cards:

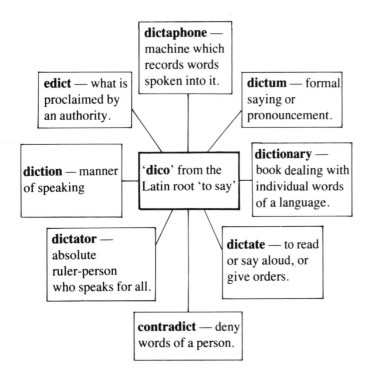

dictaphone — machine which records words spoken into it.

edict — what is proclaimed by an authority.

dictum — formal saying or pronouncement.

diction — manner of speaking

'dico' from the Latin root 'to say'

dictionary — book dealing with individual words of a language.

dictator — absolute ruler-person who speaks for all.

dictate — to read or say aloud, or give orders.

contradict — deny words of a person.

4 Make sets of cards of root words, suffixes and prefixes and play card games where children match these to make as many words as possible. Flip books could also be made in three parts with prefixes, root words and suffixes, and by flipping the pages children make as many words as possible.

5 Use dictionaries to investigate the derivatives of words.

6 Make word books based on morpheme units; for example, the morpheme 'tri', with a word on each page, including an illustration and definition:

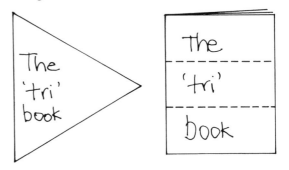

triad, triangle, triangular, tricycle, tripod, triceps, triceratops, trichotomy, tricolour, tricorn, triennial, trident, trinity, trio, triplane, triplet, trisect.

Such books may be made into flip books where the definitions and illustrations are written on the top of the page, while the word is written on the lower section. Children then flip the pages and match the word with its definition and illustration.

7 Do activities which highlight the meaning relationships between words, regardless of their pronunciation. For example:

- List related words with silent letters:

  nest, nestle

  crumble, crumb

  soft, soften

  signature, sign

  bombard, bomb.

- Complete the following words by adding missing letters:

  please, pl _ _ sant

  mean, m _ _ nt

  magic, magi _ ian

  medical, medi _ ine

  majority, maj _ _

  industrial, ind _ stry

  secretary, s _ cret.

8 Continue to develop lists of verb tenses, noting generalisations and unusual forms:

  swim, swimming, swam

  do, doing, did

  go, going, gone

  sleep, sleeping, slept.

Also note word pairs which are very similar in spelling but vary greatly in meaning and pronunciation:

  mated, matted

  mating, matting

  moped, mopped

  tiled, tilled

  filing, filling

  paled, palled.

EXTENSION ACTIVITIES FOR 'CORRECT' SPELLERS

In general, continue to develop an interest in words through activities such as the following:

1 With the children, investigate the origin of words. Words chosen for such study could include:

- words borrowed from other languages to name things originating in other countries:

coffee	—	Arabia
pizza	—	Italy
soufflé	—	France
tea	—	China
gâteau	—	France
spaghetti	—	Italy
sauerkraut	—	Germany.

In some instances the name is given according to the object's place of origin:

Brussels sprouts came from Brussels.

China (crockery) came from China.

- words derived from people's names:

  pasteurisation — named after Louis Pasteur

  braille — named after Braille

  sandwich — named after the Earl of Sandwich who did not wish to interrupt his gambling activities, so requested two slices of bread with meat between them for a meal.

- Australian words:

  boomerang, bluey, humpy.

- blended words; that is, two or more words combined to form one word:

brunch	—	breakfast/lunch
motel	—	motor/hotel
snowmobile	—	snow/automobile
handicap	—	hand in the cap.

- acronyms; that is, words formed by taking the initial letter from a number of words:

scuba	—	**s**elf **c**ontained **u**nderwater **b**reathing **a**pparatus
Qantas	—	**Q**ueensland **a**nd **N**orthern **T**erritory **A**ir **S**ervice
laser	—	**l**ight **a**mplification by **s**timulated **e**mission of **r**adiation.

- abbreviated words:

fridge	—	refrigerator
budgie	—	budgerigar
vet	—	veterinarian
phone	—	telephone
disco	—	discotheque.

- new words given to inventions and discoveries:

  polyester, nylon, sputnik.

  Note that many words also drop out of the language:

  curds and whey, gruel, victuals.

- words which are onomatopoeic; that is, echoic words which suggest their meaning because of the sound made when they are pronounced:

creak	boom
clink	cackle
crack	chant
screech	buzz
tick	clatter
giggle	chatter

  Such words could be illustrated according to their meaning:

2 Investigate the different words used to denote the same object in different parts of Australia:

> port, suitcase
>
> bathers, togs, swimmies, trunks, swimmers
>
> runners, sandshoes.

Moreover, the same word can have different meanings in different parts of Australia:

> delicatessen, scallops.

3 Set aside a time each day to discuss a 'word for the day'. Aspects such as unusual spelling patterns, origins and related words could be explored. Encourage children to use references to find information.

4 Develop word webs to explore all possible connections with a particular word:

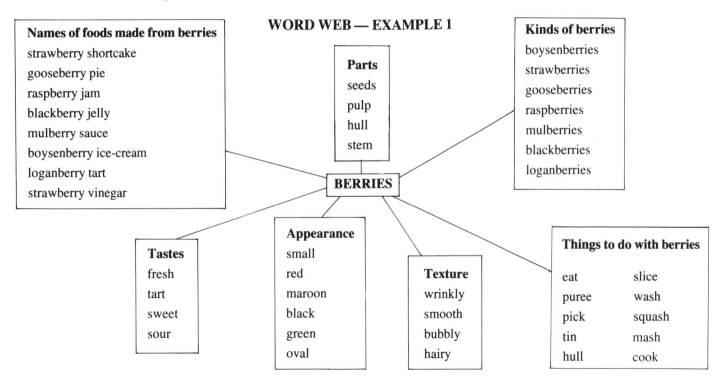

WORD WEB — EXAMPLE 1

Names of foods made from berries

strawberry shortcake

gooseberry pie

raspberry jam

blackberry jelly

mulberry sauce

boysenberry ice-cream

loganberry tart

strawberry vinegar

Parts

seeds

pulp

hull

stem

BERRIES

Kinds of berries

boysenberries

strawberries

gooseberries

raspberries

mulberries

blackberries

loganberries

Tastes

fresh

tart

sweet

sour

Appearance

small

red

maroon

black

green

oval

Texture

wrinkly

smooth

bubbly

hairy

Things to do with berries

eat	slice
puree	wash
pick	squash
tin	mash
hull	cook

WORD WEB — EXAMPLE 2

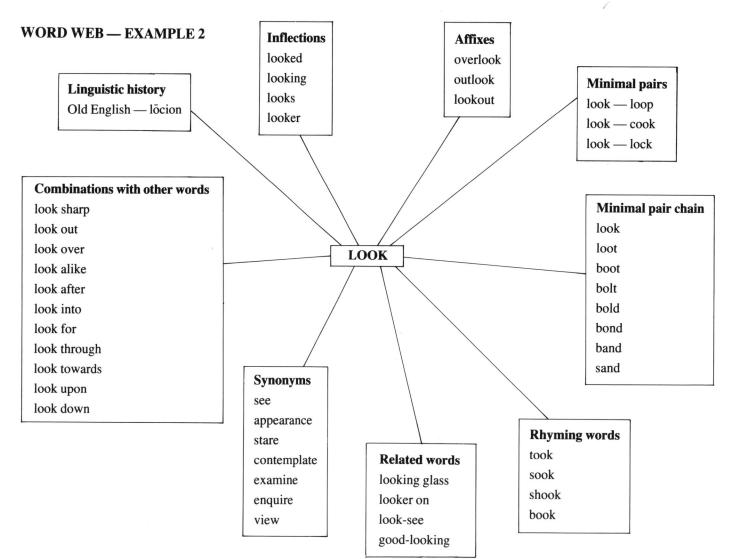

Inflections
looked
looking
looks
looker

Affixes
overlook
outlook
lookout

Linguistic history
Old English — lōcion

Minimal pairs
look — loop
look — cook
look — lock

Combinations with other words
look sharp
look out
look over
look alike
look after
look into
look for
look through
look towards
look upon
look down

LOOK

Minimal pair chain
look
loot
boot
bolt
bold
bond
band
sand

Synonyms
see
appearance
stare
contemplate
examine
enquire
view

Related words
looking glass
looker on
look-see
good-looking

Rhyming words
took
sook
shook
book

References

Fox, S. E. & Allen, V. G., *The Language Arts: An Integrated Approach*, C.B.S. College Publishing, New York, 1983.

Horn, E., 'Principles of method in teaching spelling, as derived from scientific investigation' in G. M. Whipple (ed), *Fourth report of the Committee on Economy of Time in Education*, Eighteenth Yearbook of the National Society for the Study of Education, Public School Publishing Co., Bloomington, Illinois 1919.

Ryan, D., 'Handwriting and Reading', unpublished article, Curriculum Branch, Education Department of Victoria, Carlton, 1984.

Smith, F., *Writing and the Writer*, Heinemann, London, 1982, p. 153.

6

A balanced spelling programme

Traditionally, the teaching of spelling has been through the presentation of word lists to be memorised. With the increased knowledge about the writing and spelling processes, such practice has been seriously challenged. However, in contrast, it is incorrect to assume that children will learn to spell merely through exposure to print.

Children do need to have rich interaction with written language through daily reading and writing, where every contact with print should be viewed as an opportunity to learn something new about spelling in particular, and writing in general. Some children will appear to develop with little effort a spelling 'insight' through such experiences, but even they will need help in perceiving the morphemic structure of words.

Daily time should be allocated to the teaching of spelling activities within the context of writing in all curriculum areas. Some research has suggested that the total time assigned to formal spelling be between sixty and seventy-five minutes per week. This does not mean that spelling should be seen as an isolated skill to be taught, but rather that strategies should be developed throughout each day as the most suitable opportunities arise.

According to Peters (1975) there is no question that the behaviour of teachers determines more than any other single factor whether a child does or does not learn to spell. Systematic teachers who give adequate attention to matters of spelling produce better spellers than those who leave learning to chance.

What is also important, however, is the manner in which teachers give attention to spelling.

Every contact with print should be viewed as an opportunity to learn something new about spelling

The school spelling programme

A school spelling programme should be based upon:

(a) the realisation that spelling serves writing and must be dealt with in this context. Consequently, teaching should be related to children's needs in writing rather than to external spelling lists, because words that are meaningful are more likely to be remembered.

(b) knowledge about the nature of the English orthography; that is:

- that the English orthography is highly regular
- that there are morphemic relationships between words
- that each sound is represented by a specific range of letters or letter combinations and that the position of the sound in the word will determine the likely spelling pattern
- that only particular letter sequences exist within the orthography

(c) the objectives that children will:

- become confident, competent and independent spellers who can apply acquired knowledge about the nature of the orthography to solve spelling problems, and can use resources to check attempted spellings
- be willing to take risks in their writing by attempting to spell unknown words
- develop an awareness of and interest in words

- be able to use a variety of strategies to attempt the spelling of new words
- form generalisations about the spelling of words and be prepared to constantly review and refine these generalisations
- be able to evaluate their own progress

(d) knowledge of developmental stages of spelling; that is, that most children will move through the stages of:

- precommunicative spelling
- semiphonetic spelling
- phonetic spelling
- transitional spelling
- correct spelling.

The length of time spent at any one stage and the rate of progression through these stages will vary from child to child.

(e) an awareness of the need for a language environment which is both rich and stimulating so that it provides a correct model of written language

(f) recognition of the need for both formal and incidental teaching with individuals, groups and the whole class

(g) an awareness of the importance of the children's self-esteem with regard to spelling ability. Teachers should be willing to accept spelling inventions or approximations and to highlight the positive features of such attempts, while at the same time leading the children to further understanding of the English orthography.

(h) an awareness of the value of developing independence in spelling through proof-reading, self-correcting and using appropriate resources

(i) an awareness that evaluation of spelling should be according to children's ability to use words in writing rather than to succeed in spelling tests.

The class spelling programme

The class spelling programme should facilitate the natural progression of children through the stages of development in spelling by assisting them to learn more about the nature of the English orthography. It should also help them to develop strategies for discovering the correct spelling of a required word.

In the light of the objectives listed for the school spelling programme, spelling competency in the classroom can be fostered through the following practices:

1 Provide purposeful and varied writing experiences daily: reports, stories, songs, recipes, signs, letters, lists, messages.

2 Model conventional spelling through class writing activities: class diaries, string writing, substitute writing, wall stories, class signs and instructions.

3 Provide children with an insight into the strategies *you* are using as a speller by making use of meaning relationships between words, writing a word several ways in

order to see which one looks right, using resources to check spelling, and admitting that you do not know how to spell all words.

4 Encourage children to take risks and invent spellings.

5 De-emphasise correct spelling in initial writing drafts even though published work should be spelt correctly.

6 Help pupils to develop a spelling consciousness when writing, through consideration of their future audience.

7 Develop an interest in words through word investigations (e.g. investigating word origins) and word searches (e.g. searching for words with particular patterns or features).

8 Observe and evaluate children's progress in order to intervene appropriately according to their stages of development.

9 Respond appropriately to non-standard spelling by understanding the strategies that children may be using.

10 Assist children to form generalisations about the regular nature of the English orthography.

Specific activities which focus on spelling should occur throughout each day and should total 10-15 minutes per day. Extra time should be allocated for clinic groups and individuals who require further attention.

Weekly objectives should be established for spelling, according to the needs of the individual children (as revealed in their personal writing) and the aspect of orthography that the teacher wishes to highlight. In order to integrate the spelling activities with all curriculum areas, the activities could be decided after the weekly planning of other curriculum topics. The following extract from a work programme indicates how this may be achieved:

RECORD OF PROCEDURE   Week ending: 25th May

Social Studies: Settlers following the explorers
                Focus questions – Why would settlers move to new areas?
                                  – What would new settlers take?
                                  – What would be their priorities when settling new land?

Science: Digestive system – Why do we need food?
                          – What happens to the food we eat?

Health: Social Development – co-operation with others and consideration for others.

Music: Teach song, 'I've Just Come from Sydney'

Spelling: ① Words from song – find compound words
                              – find origins of words such as 'petticoat' and 'farewell'
          ② Discuss word families related to the words 'explorers', 'settlers' and 'digestion'.
          ③ List words related to digestive system and classify in a variety of ways, noting unusual spellings, eg. 'oesophagus'
          ④ Find the meanings of the prefixes 'co' and 'con' and list other words containing these prefixes.

Effective spelling instruction requires environments in which children are encouraged to read and write extensively, and to test, evaluate and revise, if necessary, their developing theories of how the spelling system works. The learning environment for spelling is the total life environment, and the classroom spelling environment encompasses all curriculum areas.

The Place of Spelling in the School Curriculum

The following table summarises the ways in which spelling
competency is enhanced through activities in all curriculum areas.

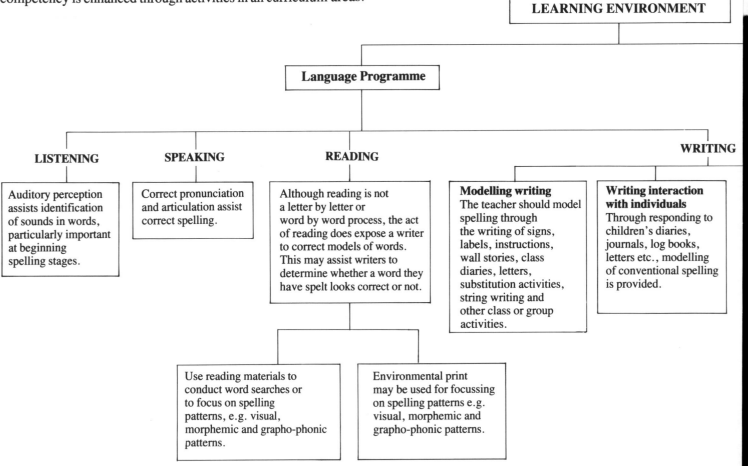

LEARNING ENVIRONMENT

Language Programme

LISTENING

Auditory perception
assists identification
of sounds in words,
particularly important
at beginning
spelling stages.

SPEAKING

Correct pronunciation
and articulation assist
correct spelling.

READING

Although reading is not
a letter by letter or
word by word process, the act
of reading does expose a writer
to correct models of words.
This may assist writers to
determine whether a word they
have spelt looks correct or not.

Use reading materials to
conduct word searches or
to focus on spelling
patterns, e.g. visual,
morphemic and grapho-phonic
patterns.

Environmental print
may be used for focussing
on spelling patterns e.g.
visual, morphemic and
grapho-phonic patterns.

WRITING

Modelling writing
The teacher should model
spelling through
the writing of signs,
labels, instructions,
wall stories, class
diaries, letters,
substitution activities,
string writing and
other class or group
activities.

**Writing interaction
with individuals**
Through responding to
children's diaries,
journals, log books,
letters etc., modelling
of conventional spelling
is provided.

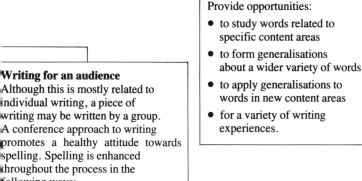

Other curriculum areas

Provide opportunities:
- to study words related to specific content areas
- to form generalisations about a wider variety of words
- to apply generalisations to words in new content areas
- for a variety of writing experiences.

Writing for an audience
Although this is mostly related to individual writing, a piece of writing may be written by a group. A conference approach to writing promotes a healthy attitude towards spelling. Spelling is enhanced throughout the process in the following ways:
- **prewriting:** rehearsing, discussing, researching (providing models and sources of words which may be used)
- **writing:** drafting, revising (allowing the writer to attempt all words), proof-reading (writer checking own spelling), editing (spelling corrected for publishing). Clinic groups may be formed for highlighting specific spelling strategies.
- **post writing:** publishing and audience response (providing a purpose for correct spelling).

The following activities elaborate on the way spelling development may be enhanced in all curriculum areas as indicated in the table, and link the stages of spelling development with appropriate activities in those curriculum areas.

In the following activities the terms are applied as follows:
- beginning spellers — precommunicative, semiphonetic stages
- developing spellers — phonetic, transitional stages
- advanced spellers — correct stage.

LANGUAGE ARTS — LISTENING

BEGINNING SPELLERS

Activities for beginning spellers include:
- listening for and identifying rhyme
- listening for and identifying initial and final sounds
- recognising repeated sounds in alliteration.

DEVELOPING SPELLERS

Activities include:
- listening and identifying medial sounds
- listening for words which contain a particular sound and identifying the symbols that represent the sound
- listening for the number of syllables in a word.

ADVANCED SPELLERS

A suggested activity is:
- listening to take notes.

This could be in the form of dictation. At the conclusion of the passage being dictated, the children must have sufficient time to proof-read, check spellings, and be sure they can make sense of what they have written. Initially the passage may be written by the children word for word as dictated, while at a later stage children may write the information in point form only.

LANGUAGE ARTS — SPEAKING

Although developing and advanced spellers rely less on phonetic strategies than beginning spellers, the pronunciation of a word still remains important, particularly if the word is unfamiliar to the speller.

To enhance clear speech, use speech rhymes in enjoyable ways from books such as *Speech Rhymes*, chosen by Clive Sansom, London, Black, 1974.

Also use opportunities in drama, poetry and choral reading activities to both model and encourage articulation.

Oral language development influences a writer's spelling as oral communication patterns are transferred into written form. This must be taken into account when observing young children's spelling of words such as 'buyed, and 'gooder' rather than the correct syntactic form. Provide ample opportunities for oral language to continue to develop through role play, drama, etc. Also provide correct models of language and positive feedback when responding to children's statements, for example:

> Child: 'I brung you some flowers.'
>
> Teacher: 'I'm glad that you brought me some flowers.'

With older students you may need to point out the correct form of a word, as children are not likely to notice mistakes when proof-reading if these mistakes merely reflect their oral language patterns.

The following example of a child's writing indicates how children's oral language influences spelling. In this particular case the child says 'th' as 'v' (note 'ver' and 'vem'). If such a speech pattern persists after the teacher judges that this developmental stage should have passed, speech therapy may be required.

One day ver was a boy and he fullnd a cave and he spent five days in it and he sor lots of Anamols and one of vem was a

Note the use of 'ver' and 'vem' for 'there' and 'them'

LANGUAGE ARTS — READING

Although we do not read letter by letter or even word by word, reading is considered to be a great influence on spelling development. Frank Smith (1984) states that we learn to spell by reading. Reading brings innumerable impressions of spelling to the brain; it is writing that impels the learner to clarify these and get the spelling correct.

The type of exposure to a range of words that children have in their reading materials will greatly influence the words they will attempt to use in their own writing. If exposure is limited to a particular set of words or word structures, this will be reflected in children's writing. Even when given the opportunity to read more widely, if only particular words are used in instructional reading time, children will perceive this as an indication of what is expected in writing. It may even influence children to become safe spellers rather than be willing to take risks with unknown words.

In the following example this seven-year-old displays his interest in dinosaurs. He had been reading books about them and has remembered the spelling of complex names even though he is still inventing the spelling of more common words:

Dinosaurs

Dinosaurs are big reptiles. The dinosuars are exsincet now because they couldnt exsist. The only kneple that were

Were alive were cave men The bigest dinosaur was the giant tryanasauras rex At that time platapusses are cald

ornithyricus wich are extinct.

The end

The reading of environmental print also influences children's spelling development. Many children are interested in the labels, signs and advertisements they see in the street, in shops and on products.

The following is an example of how aware this child is of signs in the environment:

When using reading materials for specific spelling activities, select only a couple of the following types of activities for any one text.

BEGINNING SPELLERS

In the case of beginning spellers:

- provide correct models of print in the environment by ensuring that the classroom has many signs, labels, directions, etc.
- use shared reading experiences to highlight concepts of print, such as the concept of a word and a letter, the directionality of words, and words that begin with the same letter. Children may also point out words that they recognise, or words that are used frequently.
- teach letter names
- draw attention to print in the environment when on excursions
- add high interest and high frequency words from all types of reading materials and environmental print to class word lists.

DEVELOPING SPELLERS

For developing spellers:

- continue to draw children's attention to print in the environment
- continue to add high interest and high frequency words from reading materials to class word lists
- use material read by children to conduct word searches.

Select from the following types of activities at both the phonetic and transitional stages. The activities have been devised around sample story extracts.

AT THE PHONETIC STAGE

The Boy Who Cried Wolf

There was once a boy named Peter who lived with his

grandfather. They were very poor and all they had were some sheep.

The old grandfather loved his sheep more than anything else. Every day he looked after them so that no wolf could get them.

One day he said to Peter, 'I am too old to go up the hill any more. You have grown into a big boy. I want you to take the sheep up the hill. Don't forget to look after them. They are all we have.'

Peter took the sheep up the hill where they liked to eat the green grass. He sat under a tree and looked after them.

He could see the boys and girls and dogs and cats running and playing. He saw some farmers and he saw some other people walking.

He was all by himself and he was sad.

'I want someone to play with,' he said. 'The sheep can't talk to me.'

Then one day he had an idea. While the sheep were eating the grass, Peter ran down the hill, yelling, 'Help! Help! A wolf! A wolf!'

Everyone ran up the hill to Peter. All the girls and boys ran up. All the farmers, all the dogs and all the cats and all the other people.

'Where is the wolf?' they yelled.

Peter laughed and laughed and laughed. 'It's all a joke,' he said. 'There is no wolf. I made it up.'

They didn't think Peter's idea was much of a joke. They all walked down the hill and talked angrily about him . . .

from Young Australia Anthology, Level 6, pp 36-39

1 List words with a particular initial or final sound:

/s/ — saw, some, sat, grass, cats.

Identify the symbols which represent the sound.

2 List words with a particular sound:

/f/ — grandfather, after, wolf, forget, farmers, himself, laughed, felt, myself, laughing, frighten, fattest.

Identify the symbols that represent the sound and add other words the children know containing that sound:

off, photograph, for, half, rough.

Regroup the words according to their spelling patterns:

grand**f**ather	lau**gh**ed
after	laughing
wolf	rough
forget	
farmers	o**ff**
himself	
felt	hal**f**
myself	
frighten	**ph**otograph
fattest	
for	

Use this list as a basis for adding words containing the same sound.

3 Select a word from the story and substitute letters to form new words:

dog	**d**og	**d**og
log	d**i**g	do**t**
bog	d**u**g	do**b**
fog		
hog		
jog		

4 Build words from a base word by adding or deleting a letter:

farm	ran	all
arm	an	tall

5 Provide children with a word from the story and ask children to find another word in the story that rhymes with it:

they	he	walked
day	tree	talked

AT THE TRANSITIONAL STAGE

Select from the following types of activities suggested for this piece of writing:

The Bushranger's Apprentice

Martin Jones ran away from home to become a bushranger. He knew that it would be difficult starting on his own with no experience, so he went looking for the most famous bushranger of them all, Wild Grady.

'Hand over your gold!' a voice roared out of a bunch of saplings. Wild Grady had fierce ginger whiskers and snappy eyes that could make a bunyip tremble.

'I'm sorry, but I don't have any gold, Mr Wild Grady,' Martin said politely. 'All I've got in my pocket is a clean hanky and some of Mother's home-made blackberry lollies.'

Grady was so disgusted he picked Martin up and shook him like a tablecloth, but Martin wasn't offended. 'Could I be your apprentice?' he asked.

Grady was going to answer by kicking him into the nearest prickle bush, but then he stopped to consider. It was rather lonely being a bushranger. The only people he ever met were ones he held up at pistol point, and the conversations he had with them weren't exactly chatty.

'All right,' he said. 'But only on a trial. If you don't measure up, then — PHWTTT!' He drew his finger across his throat in a very descriptive manner. His camp was messy. He had a tatty old tent made out of stolen mailbags, and some really horrible stew in a pot that needed a good scrubbing.

'Stay by the track, keep your eyes open, and don't come back empty handed,' he told Martin, handing him a spare pistol.

Martin didn't have long to wait. A man came down the track from the gold fields, with a bag over his shoulder.

'Hand over your gold!' Martin said, brandishing the pistol. 'I represent Wild Grady!'

The man sank to his knees at the mention of that name.

'I'm only a poor digger,' he said nervously. 'I've got

a wife and ten kids to support. This gold was to buy me wife a nice little washtub as she has to do all the washing in the creek, the roof of my hut leaks, I've got sciatica something awful, our horse ran away, someone stole our cow so we haven't got any milk for our porridge. Every time I find a nice little nugget or two, a bushranger leaps out and takes it off me. It's hard work, fossicking, and no means to protect myself, either. I'm too poor to afford a pistol.'

Martin was so moved he said, 'You'd better take this pistol, then. And I'm sorry I troubled you.'

'In return you can have this sack of gold nuggets,' the man said gratefully, and ran off down the track.

Martin took the bag to Grady's hideout and told him what had happened. He emptied the bag upside down, but it wasn't full of gold nuggets. It was full of sample bottles of hair restorer.

Grady was fierce enough when in an ordinary mood, but when he was in a rage, he looked like something nasty out of an old legend . . .

from Young Australia Anthology, Level 14, pp 74-75

1 Note spelling of 'sciatica'. List, or find in a dictionary, other words where 'sc' is /s/:

science, scissors, scythe, scintillate.

2 List words with an /ay/ sound:

away, bushranger, Grady, made, tablecloth, wait, name, came, takes, gratefully, rage, stay.

Classify them according to visual patterns:

a**way**	bushra**nger**	ma**de**
stay	Grady	name
	tablecloth	came
w**ait**		takes
		gratefully
		rage

Ask children to suggest other words with the same sound and add these to the visual groupings. Identify the symbols that represent the sound.

3 Note the silent 'k' in the word 'knee'. List other words with the same pattern:

know, knowledge, knife, knock, knit, knob, knight, kneel, knick-nack, knapsack, knead, knot, knoll, knuckle.

Also note the silent 'w' in 'answer'.

4 Find words ending with 'le':

tremble, trouble, prickle, horrible, little.

5 Find words within the word 'bushranger':

bush, ranger, range, ran, bus, anger, an, rang.

6 Use the letters of the word 'bushranger' to make other words:

hang, rag, nag, sag, bag, shrub, rub, usher, bug, rug, hug, shrug, sang, rang, bang, rare, hare, bare, rear, gear, sear, hear, he, are, near, bear, she, shear, rush, bush, gush, grab.

Regroup the words according to spelling patterns:

rag	**near**	**rare**
nag	bear	hare
sag	gear	bare
bag	rear	
	sear	
	hear	

Regroup according to sound patterns:

rare	near
bear	gear
hare	rear
	sear
	hear

7 Find words with the suffix 'ing':

starting, looking, kicking, brandishing, washing, fossicking.

Identify the base word in each case (for example, 'kick') and build other words on this base:

kicked, kicker.

Continue to add to this list of 'ing' words from other sources and encourage children to form generalisations; for example, doubling the consonant when the word has a short vowel sound:

hop, hopping, hopped.

8 List compound words:

bushranger, blackberry, home-made, tablecloth, mailbags, washtub, myself, hideout, something.

Identify the words within each compound word and where appropriate build up other words based on these:

myself, yourself, himself, herself.

9 Note the spelling of 'all right' as two words, and encourage children to develop their own mnemonics:

'All right' is spelt as two words like 'all wrong'.

10 List contractions, identify the component words, and note what the apostrophe is representing:

I'm, I've, didn't, weren't, don't, haven't, it's, wasn't, you'd.

Continue to add to this list as other contractions are found.

11 Use words within the story to play letter change activities; for example, 'said' to 'told':

said

sa _ d

_ and

b _ nd

bo _ d

_ old

ADVANCED SPELLERS

When working with advanced spellers:

- draw attention to print in the environment, particularly noting:

    incorrect spellings (unintentional):
    > CUPACCINO, SANWICHES

    incorrect spellings (intentional):
    > RITE-WAY, TONITE, CITICHEAP, TRANZACTION CARD

    misuse of homophones as a play on words:
    > MANE EVENT (hairdresser), RIGHT SIGNS (signwriter)

- continue to add high frequency and high interest words from reading materials to class word lists.
- use material read by children to conduct word searches. Select from the following types of activities suggested for this piece of writing:

No Space in Space

Scientists have worked out that if a satellite is 35,680 kilometres from the Earth directly above the equator, it will orbit at the same speed as the rotation of the Earth. This means that the satellite will always be above the same fixed point on Earth. Every country wants to have communication satellites travelling in this orbit to transfer information and pictures twenty-four hours a day.

There are also polar-orbiting satellites which pass over the North and South Poles, taking about 100 minutes to make one orbit of the Earth.

One problem that may arise is the overcrowding of orbit paths. Methods will have to be worked out to prevent this . . . possibly satellites will be sent higher — but then they'll have to use stronger signals to reach Earth; perhaps fewer but larger satellites will be sent into orbit. It might even be your job in the future to work on this very problem!

Although satellite communication seems foolproof, scientists are testing another efficient system which would use a new kind of cable under the sea. The cables would be made of optical fibres — hair-fine glass fibres which transmit signals from a laser. It is considered just as important to keep making technological advances in cable communication as it is in satellite communication, as the two systems provide a backup for each other. If something that we can't even imagine did happen to the world's satellite system, we would at least still be able to contact other countries by the cable network. Similarly, if the cable network was destroyed or damaged, there is a good chance that we could still use the satellites.

Satellites are helping to make telecommunications so easy and fast that people all over the world can be aware of triumphs and disasters as soon as they occur.

Special Landsat satellites can track pollution, see if

crops are diseased, and spot underground water sources. These special satellites circle the Earth fourteen times a day in a near-polar orbit. They shift slightly to the west each time they orbit, making one complete observation of the Earth every eighteen days. Landsat transmits messages to Earth, where computers change them into special photographic images. These images can give us information that normal photographs cannot show.

Other polar-orbit satellites watch the oceans, lakes and rivers. They can monitor the movement of sea-life: porpoises, whales, turtles and many fishes. These satellites can keep track of icebergs and warn ships of any danger they might cause.

From high up in space, satellites observe what is happening on Earth and relay the information back through computers to receiving stations here.

Computers then translate the information into a form that is useful to us.

The stations on Earth have antennae which receive and send satellite signals. The antennae are in the centre of bowl-shaped collectors called dishes . . .

from Satellites in Space, *Young Australia, Level 16*

1 Children could find the meanings of the derivatives of words, and build lists of words based on such derivatives:

kilo**metre**

kilogram	peri**meter**
kilowatt	deci**metre**
kilojoule	centi**metre**
kilotonne	alti**meter**
	metric
	thermo**meter**
	baro**meter**
	metrology

Other such words to be located include:

equator, rotation, polar, orbit, translate, transfer, transmit, optical, technological, circle, photographic.

2 Locate compound words:

iceberg, foolproof, overcrowding, backup, network, something, underground, sea-life.

Build word lists based on these:

foolproof

foolhardy	water**proof**
	proofread
	sound**proof**

underground

underneath	**ground**work
underwear	**ground**keeper
undergrowth	**ground**cover
underhand	

3 Find the derivation of 'laser' (acronym).

4 List words to note comparatives and superlatives:

strong, stronger, strongest

large, larger, largest

high, higher, highest

few, fewer, fewest.

Continue to add to this list from other sources so that generalisations can be formed.

5 Note regular word endings:

ion	**or**
station	equator
communication	monitor
information	collector
rotation	
observation	
pollution	

Form generalisations about the types of words which have these endings.

6 Note plural forms:

country, countries

antenna, antennae

dish, dishes.

7 List words ending in 'ing':

travelling	making
orbiting	overcrowding
taking	helping

Note the base word for each of these words; for example, making — make. Continue to add to this list from other resources and form generalisations about how to add 'ing'. In particular note the spelling of 'orbiting'.

8 Select words from which word families can be built:

efficient	**use**	**easy**
inefficient	unusable	easily
efficiency	usable	ease
efficiently	useful	disease
deficient	misuse	easiness
	useless	easier
	abuse	easiest
	user	uneasily
	usefully	
	disuse	

9 List words containing a particular sound:

/or/ — orbit, warn, always, information, twenty-four, also, north, although, your, for, all, sources, normal.

Identify the symbols that represent the sound, add to the list from other sources, and regroup according to spelling patterns.

10 Identify words which are homophones. List these words with their homophones:

here, hear

warn, worn

sources, saucers

11 List words which are homographs and find the alternative meanings for such:

will, means, watch, pass.

12 Have children select words to play games such as Hangman, with players encouraging their partners to predict the missing letters according to serial probability:

_ _ _ _ k   (track).

LANGUAGE ARTS — WRITING

BEGINNING SPELLERS

MODELLING WRITING

Model writing in a variety of ways (see pages 24-28) as this will present correct spellings to children. When modelling or writing in front of the children, do not be afraid to admit that you do not know how to spell a word.

Ways of modelling conventional spelling include:

1 **Wall stories, class diary**:

Yesterday we went to the zoo. We saw some bears, elephants, gorillas, giraffes, monkeys, camels, snakes and zebras. We had lunch on the lawn outside the cafe. We took some photos of the animals. The funniest thing that happened was when the elephant squirted water all over Mrs. Smith. We had a lovely day.

While writing, the teacher should incidentally discuss the following points:

- where to begin the sentence
- the direction of print
- where a word begins and ends
- the spaces between words.

The wall story could later be used for:

- counting the number of words in a sentence
- finding words which begin with a particular letter
- substitution activities:

> We had a ＿＿ day.
>
> We had a **fun** day.
>
> We had a **tiring** day.
>
> We had a **happy** day.
>
> We had an **exciting** day.

Encourage children to write their own stories about the topic.

2 **Substitution of words in an author's structure**

Select a rhyme or poem and substitute alternative words within the rhyme according to children's suggestions:

> Mary Mary, quite contrary
>
> How does your garden grow?
>
> With silver bells and cockle shells
>
> And pretty maids all in a row.
>
> ＿＿＿ ＿＿ quite contrary
>
> How does your garden grow?
>
> With ＿＿ ＿＿ and ＿＿ ＿＿
>
> And ＿＿ ＿＿ all in a row.

Substitute the children's suggestions in this structure, writing each one on a chart or compiling the different verses into a book for later reading activities.

3 **Expanded sentences**

Select a sentence from children's own writing or class writing, or from material read by the children and expand it in the following way:

> I like to ride my bike.
>
> I like to ride my **new** bike.
>
> I like to ride my new **red** bike.

The words of the original sentence may be written on cards so that the sentence is readily expanded with new word cards.

4 **String writing**

Begin with a topic word and list words which describe the topic word according to children's suggestions:

> dirty   **pigs**
>
> pink
>
> fat
>
> baby
>
> mother

Then ask what pigs do and list these:

> **pigs**   snort
>
>   eat
>
>   sleep
>
>   waddle
>
>   roll.

Children then string the words together to form a sentence:

Fat pigs waddle.

These can be written on sentence strips for later reading.

Another form of string writing

5 Write classroom signs, labels, directions, etc. in front of the children.

WRITING FOR AN AUDIENCE

Encourage children to write daily, inventing their own spelling (see pages 22 and 28). Continue to nurture their belief in their ability to write by not focussing attention on correct spelling.

Some children may be reluctant to begin writing and especially to attempt invented spelling having been conditioned before starting school to believe that they are not able to spell according to conventional adult standards. This may be overcome by praising other children's attempts as well as involving the hesitant children in substitution activities. Any attempt to make marks on paper should be praised as writing and displayed as such in the classroom.

Other children may wish to write using symbols but be unable to produce the intended letters, particularly in the semiphonetic stage. Such children may like to have an alphabet frieze to refer to on their desk or table.

Some children may remain at the precommunicative stage for such a long period that you may feel the need to intervene to assist them to develop word concepts and the beginning of sound/symbol relationships. For such children the following technique could be used:

• Work with the child writing a blank for each word in the child's story as it is told to you:

_____ ____ _____ ____ ____

- For each word, encourage the child to listen for any sounds heard in the word and to record such sounds in the matching blank space.

Some children are not willing to write more than one or two lines of writing. In some instances this is merely because the child is only provided with one piece of paper, but it may also occur if teacher modelling is limited to 'a class sentence' per day for language experience activities or handwriting activities. Extended writing is more likely to occur if the child is given a number of pages stapled together and is encouraged to write more than one page. Class writing should include wall stories and other extended writing. Children can also be encouraged to read their writing to each other with listener questioning the writer. The writer may then see the need to add further information.

DEVELOPING SPELLERS

MODELLING WRITING
Model writing in a variety of ways (see pp. 24 to 28) as this will present correct spellings to children. Ways of modelling include:

1 **Wall story, class diary**
Using the previous wall story on page 70:

- identify words with an /f/ sound:

    elephants, giraffes, cafe, photos, funniest

    and isolate the symbols that represent the sound. Add these words to your class alphabet word lists or word banks.

- identify words which have the same visual patterns and list these together:

s**aw**	happ**en**ed	yester**day**
l**aw**n	wh**en**	**day**
	w**en**t	

- Locate words which appear more than once:

    some, we, the.

    Refer to them on your class word list of high frequency words.

- Expand sentences and substitute words:

    Yesterday we went to the zoo.

    Yesterday we went to the zoo by bus.

    Yesterday we travelled to the zoo in the morning.

    We had a lovely day.

    We had a lovely day because we were away from school.

2 **String writing**
Extend string writing activities by asking additional questions, such as *what*, *where*, *when* and *why*:

pigs					
	roll		in the mud	every day	because they like being dirty.
	eat	noisily	in their pen	when they are hungry.	

3 **Substitution** of words in an author's structure:

> There was an old lady
> Who swallowed a fly
> I wonder why she swallowed a fly
> Poor old lady, I think she'll die.

> There was an old man
> Who swallowed a book
> I wonder why he swallowed a book
> Poor old man, I think he's crook.

Words which are substituted must rhyme but not necessarily have the same spelling pattern (e.g. fly, die). This may also be done with stories which have a repetitive pattern.

WRITING INTERACTION WITH INDIVIDUALS

Ways of interacting with children's writing include:

1 **Written conversations**

These take place between the child and a teacher, or another adult or older child who is a competent speller. The child begins by writing a statement to which the teacher responds by asking a question. The child then responds to that question.

Continue in this way for a few statements and questions and conclude with the child reading all statements and questions. This can also be done with a small group moving from child to child within the group.

> We went to the zoo
> and saw the grafs.
> What did the giraffes look like?
> The girraffes were very talle
> What makes giraffes so tall?
> The giraffes have long neks.
> Why do they need long necks?
> Their necks can strehc
> over the fens.

An example of a written conversation

2 Letters, journals or diaries

Respond to children's letters in writing. Although the message of the writer is the most important factor, opportunities will arise for presenting correct models of misspelt words.

> Dear Mrs Smith,
> Last night I went to cubs. I got a sertificat for tieing notts. My dad was very prowed of me.
> Yours sincerely,
> Paul
>
> Dear Paul,
> Congratulations on receiving your special certificate for tying knots. I am very proud of you too. Are you going to frame your certificate? Perhaps you could bring it to school and show us how to tie some knots.
> Yours sincerely,
> Mrs Smith.

Note that correct models of spelling are provided without detracting from the personal interest in the child. In the child's subsequent reply it is more likely that the correct spelling will be used. This method is a positive means of supplying correct spelling without denigrating the writer.

WRITING FOR AN AUDIENCE

Encourage children to write daily. When children are writing, their first drafts may contain spelling mistakes, and in fact the children should be encouraged to take risks and attempt to spell words they are unsure of. Discourage children from asking how to spell words and insist that they attempt to spell the words themselves. Advice should only be given after children have attempted the spelling.

If using the conference approach to writing, the initial conferences should concentrate on the content of the writing rather than the surface features such as spelling. However, spelling should be dealt with before the writing is published to ensure that published works contain correct spelling. Even if not using this approach to writing, the correction of spelling errors should occur in the following ways:

1 Children proof-read their writing, looking for errors. Note that children in the phonetic and transitional stages may only be able to correct known words and may not be able to correct attempted spellings. They may still be at a stage where they are not sure whether a word 'looks right' or not. Consequently they may even think that a correctly spelt word is incorrect. The important consideration at this stage is to develop the *habit* of proof-reading.

Children proof-read by underlining the words they think are misspelt. When proof-reading, children may:

- instantly correct those words which are misspelt but which are really known words
- underline other words recognised as being misspelt but which the children may not be able to correct
- not recognise some misspelt words
- underline correctly spelt words because they think they are wrong.

The words which are misspelt but not underlined indicate those words with which children need greater assistance.

2 Note which words have been underlined and assist the children in the following ways:

- Indicate those words which are spelt correctly, perhaps by ticking the word.

- In the case of words that you consider the children should know (which may be on 'Words I Know' cards or in personal word books), encourage them to correct the spelling.

- For words the children may not be expected to know, direct them to class word lists or other resources, if possible, to find the correct spellings. Ask the children if there are any words they would particularly like to learn how to spell. Only select a limited number of such words. Write the words for them and tell them to use the 'look, say, cover, write, check' method of copying and remembering the word (see page 32). At the same time, you may teach words with a similar spelling pattern or words which are related. These words should be added to the children's personal word lists.

- Other words may be corrected by the person who types the children's work for publication, or by the class editorial board. If the children are to rewrite their pieces for publication, you will need to model the correct spellings for the children to copy. This may be done by the teacher or other competent spellers.

You may wish to establish an editorial board in the classroom, to which the writer submits work to be published. This editorial board may be a group of competent spellers or a changing group of mixed ability which is responsible for a set period of time for editing work to be published. The editors should discuss the piece of writing with the author to ensure that the author is satisfied with any decisions made. Remember that the ownership of the writing still belongs with the author.

When making decisions about the number of words to be self-corrected, the teacher must consider both the ability of the child and the onerous nature of the task. It is important that children do not lose their interest in writing or their willingness to attempt the spelling of unknown words. The main purposes of the suggestions outlined above are to encourage independence in writing and to provide a strategy for learning new words.

3 Clinic or focus groups may be formed during a writing session to assist specifically with spelling, particularly if a group of children have a common problem. For example:

- at the phonetic stage, a group of children may not be listening to identify the sounds they hear in words

- at the transitional stage, a group of children may be overgeneralising in their use of the silent 'e' in words such as 'bake' (back) and 'slepe' (sleep).

4 Words from children's personal writing may be added to class words lists.

Example of a piece of writing and how the writer may be assisted:

r chiner

, my grad is chineys his name is

od rang fore sharr we kole him E.T.

The Tar has enjyshots.

This is about China.
A boy in my grade is Chinese. His name is Edward Tang.
For short we call him E.T. That are his initials.

(a) Check words underlined and point out that 'short' was correct. Tick this word.

(b) The child should attempt to spell words that the teacher considers should be known. This may be done on a 'have a go' card. For example:

1st try	2nd try	3rd try	Correct model	Child's copy
floor	for			for
aer	are			are
grayd	graid	graed	grade	grade

The correct model is provided by the teacher if the child's attempts are still incorrect.

(c) Ask the child to check a sign in classroom to confirm the spelling of 'grade' and to check the class word list of high frequency words to confirm the spelling of 'for' and 'are'. These words may also be in the child's personal alphabetical word book. Relate the spelling of 'grade' to a known word of similar pattern, e.g. 'made'. Ask the child about other words which may contain the same spelling pattern, e.g. trade, spade, fade, and write these for the child. If such a pattern exists in a word list in class, refer to this.

(d) Indicate the words spelt incorrectly that have not been underlined.

(e) Ask the child which of these misspelt words he would like to learn to spell, e.g. 'China', 'Chinese', 'Edward', 'initials'. (Be sure that the child does not choose too many.) Refer the child to Edward himself as a resource for 'Edward' 'China' and 'Chinese'. Write the four words on the child's 'have a go' card and have the child practise these, using the 'look, say, cover, write, check' method. The child should write these words in a personal alphabetical word book.

(f) Find out from the child which word was intended instead of 'thet' (that), encouraging the child to use the correct word (they).

(g) Correct other words underlined ('about' and 'call') for the child by writing the correct form above each word, if the child intends to rewrite this piece for publication.

(h) Add the child's suggested word(s) to class word lists encouraging the child to consider which of the words may be useful to other writers, e.g. 'call'.

ADVANCED SPELLERS

Use the same procedures outlined for developing spellers, but expect the children to thoroughly proof-read their own work and to use a variety of resources to confirm spelling. When they are attempting unknown words, encourage them to relate these words to known words using morphemic, visual and phonetic strategies.

OTHER CURRICULUM AREAS

Throughout the day, make use of opportunities to foster an interest in words and to note the spelling of words which highlight aspects of the English orthography and may be added to particular class word lists.

EXAMPLE TOPIC: TIME
The following words may occur during oral and written discussions on the topic of time, and the suggested spelling activities are indicated:

BEGINNING SPELLERS

morning	midnight	birthday
afternoon	sunrise	Christmas
clock	sunset	calendar
watch	yesterday	daylight
hands	Easter	sunlight
day	holiday	moonlight
night	Monday	today
daytime	Tuesday etc.	tomorrow

night-time	lunch time	week
Spring	play time	month
Summer	midday	year
Winter	before	weekend
Autumn	after	o'clock

Suggested activities:
- Look for words which begin with the same letter.
- Listen for words which begin with the same sound.
- Listen for words with a particular sound, e.g. Christmas, calendar, clock, week.
- Listen for words with the same ending, e.g. holiday, Monday, birthday, yesterday.
- Listen for words with the same beginning, e.g. today, tomorrow; sunrise, sunset.
- Use the words in statements or wall stories about the topic.
- Provide songs, books and rhymes about time for children to read.
- Encourage children to write their own statements or stories about the topic.

DEVELOPING SPELLERS

Use the previous words plus:

hour	timetable	full moon
second	estimate	crescent

minute	leap year	half moon
during	shadow	daylight saving
throughout	hour glass	egg-timer
breakfast	sundial	sand clock
dinner	candle clock	fortnight
brunch	water clock	season
lunch	darkness	noon
tea	ticking	dusk
alarm	cuckoo clock	dawn
digital	grandfather clock	clockwork
stop watch		

Suggested activities:

- Note words with capital letters.
- Note that 'minute' may be said in two different ways (homograph).
- Listen for sounds in the middle of words.
- Note opposites in meaning, e.g. dusk, dawn; before, after.
- Note compound words.
- Note derivation of words:

    fortnight — fourteen days

    breakfast — break fast

    brunch — breakfast/lunch.

- Build up word families, e.g. tick, ticking, ticked, ticks, ticker.

- Note words within words, e.g. season: sea, son, as, on, seas.
- Note words with a particular spelling pattern, e.g. 'ea': tea, leap, season, breakfast.
- Note words with a particular sound e.g. /ar/: half, alarm, grandfather, darkness, hour glass.

ADVANCED SPELLERS

Use the previous words plus:

centenary	century
decade	seasonal
bicentenary	pendulum
annual	oscillate
perennial	Eastern Standard Time
eclipse	estimate
monthly	atomic clock
bimonthly	time line
fortnightly	Greenwich Mean Time
duration	International date line
quartz	Estimated Time of Arrival (e.t.a.)
biannual	a.m.
half yearly	p.m.
annually	period
quarterly	rate
financial year	phase
era	anniversary

Suggested activities:

- Note abbreviations, e.g. a.m., p.m., e.t.a., and check the derivation of these.
- Develop word families, e.g. century, centenary, centennial, bicentenary. Relate other words, e.g. cent, percent, percentage.
- Find out origins of names of days of week, names of months, special times, etc.
- Group words with the same derivation, e.g. bicentenary, bimonthly, biannual.
- Note suffixes, e.g. 'at', 'ly', 'ary'.
- Note unusual spellings, e.g. oscillate, crescent, autumn.
- Locate words in stories, magazines, newspapers, etc.

THE DEVELOPMENT AND USE OF CLASS WORD LISTS

It is vital in a spelling programme to develop class word lists and to draw attention to such lists in a variety of ways and for a variety of purposes throughout the day in all curriculum areas. These lists should be added to, refined and modified according to needs at particular times.

Word lists should be developed from:

- children's personal reading and writing
- class or group topic work
- class or group reading or writing activities
- individual word books.

They should contain:

- high frequency words (See Appendix 1)
- high interest words
- words children require for their writing
- words that children commonly misspell
- words that highlight features of the English orthography.

They should be used for:

- confirming attempted spellings
- formation and review of generalisations
- focussing on particular features of the English orthography — morphemic, visual and phonetic patterns
- classification purposes, e.g. alphabetical order, topics and subtopics
- expansion of children's vocabularies.

The most important aspect of word lists is the type of activities for which they are used. The same topic word list may be developed in an infant grade and an upper primary grade, but the activities for both groups would need to be different because the children would be using different strategies for spelling.

Types of word lists may include (depending on the stage of development of the children):

- alphabetical
- sound grouping
- visual pattern grouping

- prefixes and suffixes
- derivatives
- compound words
- acronyms (words formed from the initial letters of words)
- homophones (words which sound the same, but are spelt differently)
- palindromes (words spelt the same forwards or backwards)
- high frequency words
- synonyms and antonyms
- eponyms (words derived from the name of a person or place)
- homographs (words which have the same spelling but may be pronounced differently and have different meanings)
- portmanteau words (words made by combining the parts of two words)
- anagrams (words which are made up of the same group of letters).

These class lists are not for the purpose of rote memory of words. However they can be a source from which children select a number of words to be learned within a short period of time if the children choose to do so. If used in this way, the children choose the number of words to be learned, which words will be learned and when they will be learned by. Some children particularly enjoy this challenge and because the words are meaningful to them they will use them more readily in their personal writing.

PUBLISHED WORD LISTS

Such lists should not be used for rote memory tasks for spelling as they may include:

- words the children may not wish to use in their writing
- words the children already know how to spell

and they may *not* include words the children need for their writing.

Moreover, the children will not necessarily transfer their learning of the spelling of words in published lists to the spelling of words in their written language. However, published word lists may serve useful purposes if they are:

- used for word searches which highlight features of the English orthography, e.g. a word search for compound words
- used by children to confirm attempted spellings.

Some word lists may even be useful to help form generalisations about plurals, comparatives and superlatives, and verb tenses, as well as to provide information about homophones, contractions and alternative spellings.

EXAMPLES OF WHAT MAY BE DONE WITH PUBLISHED WORD LISTS

Example 1: from the Salisbury Word List (South Australia), Group 201-300 (4% of words used in children's writing — Years 3-7).

much	right	most	island
stopped	set	red	run
decided	finished	world	oh
five	hour	boys	ate
here	knew	caught	behind
few	o'clock	dead	breakfast
money	brother	every	earth
always	coming	live	flying
horse	I'm	lost	front
year	make	new	hot
days	story	opened	liked
family	under	ten	same
really	wanted	window	give
also	any	woke	love
great	food	half	birthday
it's	outside	minutes	eat
think	thing	everyone	hours
tried	many	jumped	Mars
want	tea	stay	mouse
couldn't	ground	baby	reached
dark	John	lady	road
head	sat	lots	eyes
walk	work	pageant	kept
fire	best	played	both
four	life	beach	green

Suggested activities are as follows:

1 Find words in the past tense. List these with other verb tenses:

stopped:	stop, stopping, stopped
decided:	decide, deciding, decided
tried:	try, trying, tried
finished:	finish, finishing, finished
wanted:	want, wanting, wanted
opened:	open, opening, opened
sat:	sit, sitting, sat
caught:	catch, catching, caught
lost:	lose, losing, lost
jumped:	jump, jumping, jumped
played:	play, playing, played
ate:	eat, eating, ate
liked:	like, liking, liked
reached:	reach, reaching, reached
kept:	keep, keeping, kept

Form generalisations about the present participle and the past tense (when to double the consonant, when to delete the 'e'). Note unusual forms of the past tenses.

2 Search for compound words. List these, separate them into component elements and build up related word lists:

outside: beside, sidewalk, outlook, outdoors . . .

everyone: everybody, someone . . .

breakfast: windbreak, break-in, steadfast . . .

birthday: birthmark, daylight, Monday . . .

3 List contractions and write complete words:

    couldn't: could not

    o'clock: of the clock

    I'm: I am

    it's: it is

4 List words with a particular sound:

    /u/: much, brother, coming, under, everyone, money, jumped, front, love, run.

Regroup them according to spelling patterns.

5 Note interesting spellings, e.g. pageant, island, knew.

6 Develop a comparative and superlative chart using appropriate words from the list:

few	———	———
dark	———	———
———	———	best
———	———	most
red	———	———
new	———	———
hot	———	———
green	———	———

7 Note homophones, e.g. knew, new.

8 List other words with the prefix 'be':

before, befall, behalf, behold, bedraggled, begin, believe, belated, belong, below, bemused, beside, become . . .

Example 2: from *The Australian Writer's Wordbook*, Thomas Nelson, 1984

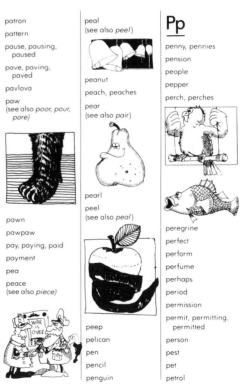

patron

pattern

pause, pausing, paused

pave, paving, paved

pavlova

paw (see also *poor, pour, pore*)

pawn

pawpaw

pay, paying, paid

payment

pea

peace (see also *piece*)

peal (see also *peel*)

peanut

peach, peaches

pear (see also *pair*)

pearl

peel (see also *peal*)

peep

pelican

pen

pencil

penguin

Pp

penny, pennies

pension

people

pepper

perch, perches

peregrine

perfect

perform

perfume

perhaps

period

permission

permit, permitting, permitted

person

pest

pet

petrol

Suggested activities are as follows:

1 Use the list to check the spelling of homophones, e.g. paw, peace, peel.

2 Use the list to form generalisations about verb tenses:

    pause, pausing, paused

    pave, paving, paved

    pay, paying, paid

    permit, permitting, permitted.

3 Form generalisations about plurals:

    peach, peaches

    perch, perches

    penny, pennies.

4 List compound words:

    pawpaw, peanut.

5 Find words within words:

    pen in the words pencil, penguin, penny, pension

    pea in the words peace, peanut, peal, peach, pear, pearl

    paw in the words pawpaw, pawn.

6 Note different meanings of one word, e.g. perch.

7 Note the word 'pavlova' and ask children to find out about its origin.

8 Build up a word family based on a word:

    person: personable, personal, personally, personality, personalise, personify, personnel, personification.

As children's spelling development can be influenced greatly by the print in their environment, the value of word lists cannot be underestimated. Reference to word lists can provide children with the opportunity to test, evaluate and revise, if necessary, their developing theories of how the spelling system works.

References

Peters, M.L., *Diagnostic and Remedial Spelling Manual*, London, Macmillan, 1975.

Smith, F., 'Demonstrations, Engagement, and Sensitivity' in F. Smith, *Essays Into Literacy*, Heinemann Educational, Exeter, New Hampshire, 1983.

7

...ment

...and

...ation

Assessment of spelling involves the gathering of information about the spelling performance of children for the purposes of making comparisons or making an evaluation.

Evaluation of spelling is the interpretation of such assessments for the purpose of planning future instruction.

Spelling assessment should be viewed within the total language context and especially within the context of writing. It should be continuous and based upon a range of experiences throughout all curriculum areas. In using children's writing as an indication of their spelling competence, it is necessary to systematically observe a number of pieces of writing at any one time.

The overall assessment should be related to both children's attitudes to, and competence in, spelling. It should not be gauged according to the children's ability to memorise words, but rather should be gauged by observing the spelling processes they use when writing.

When assessing spelling, correctness is not the one and only consideration. Correct spelling, as with all aspects of correct written language, must be seen as a long term goal and not something that can be taught in one year. So progress in spelling development, with approximations becoming gradually more like conventional spelling, is the important aspect to assess.

The teaching programme and materials being used should be evaluated in relation to the school policy and its philosophy of learning about spelling. Children should also become involved in self-evaluation.

Means of assessment

Assessment of children's spelling may occur in the following ways:

1 OBSERVATION

Aspects to be observed are:

- a willingness to attempt to spell unknown words
- the child's self-image in matters relating to spelling
- an interest in words
- a willingness to use a range of resources, e.g. class word lists, published word lists, dictionaries, other people, reading material
- evidence of a 'spelling consciousness'; that is, being aware of a sense of audience and consequently spelling as well as possible
- ability to form generalisations from word lists
- development of a systematic method for attempting to learn new words
- efficiency and speed in writing words.

2 COLLECTING SAMPLES OF CHILDREN'S WRITING

Samples of writing should be collected and dated on a regular basis throughout the year. At any one time, a number of pieces of writing should be collected. If possible, these samples should be drawn from writing for a variety of different purposes. They should also include some initial drafts as well as proof-read material. It is important to have samples of writing in which children attempt unknown words in order to analyse their spelling strategies.

Aspects which may be assessed are:

- strategies children are using when attempting unknown words (morphemic, visual and phonetic strategies) which enable us to note their stage of development
- children's knowledge of concepts of print, i.e. directionality, knowledge of words and letters
- the accumulation of a known body of words
- the ability to apply generalisations
- children's willingness to proof-read according to their stage of development
- their willingness to use invented spellings or approximations
- an individual's specific needs in spelling
- an individual's spelling progress
- whether or not some errors are habitual and consistent.

3 EXAMINING CHILDREN'S INDIVIDUAL RECORDS

Individual records to examine include 'have a go' cards, personal word lists and word books.

Aspects to be observed are:

- strategies for trying unknown words
- the types of words children are interested in learning
- children's willingness to independently correct words.

4 A SPELLING INTERVIEW

You may wish to use a spelling interview at the beginning of the school year to ascertain the children's attitudes and approaches to spelling, or you may wish only to give this to children encountering difficulty with spelling. Although it is time-consuming to give such an interview, it is worthwhile because of the spelling insights it reveals. The interview could include questions such as:

1 When you're writing and come to a word you don't know how to spell, what do you do?

2 Do you ever do anything else?

3 Who do you know who are good spellers and what makes them good spellers?

4 Do you think they ever meet a word they don't know how to spell?

5 What do you think they do then?

6 If you knew someone was having difficulty spelling a word, how would you help them?

7 What if that didn't help?

8 What would the teacher do to help that person?

9 Who helped you learn to spell?

10 Is it possible to learn to spell by yourself? How?

11 Do you think you are improving as a speller? Why?

12 Do you think you're a good speller? Why?

13 What is a 'tricky' word?

14 Do you ever see words in the environment that are misspelt?

15 Do you like writing/spelling?

16 Is learning to spell easy/hard? Why?

17 Are there any words you have learnt to spell from books you have read?

18 Are there any words you have learnt to spell from watching TV?

19 Are there any words you can spell after having seen them in a shop, etc.?

20 Do you know what a word is? Tell/Show me.

21 Do you know what a letter is? Tell/Show me.

22 How would you copy a word?

23 Does it matter if you spell a word wrongly?

24 How do you feel when the teacher marks your work wrong?

25 Do you need to learn how to spell? Why?

26 Is there a proper way to spell a word?

27 How do you learn to spell a particular word?

28 What is a dictionary?

29 Do you use a dictionary? Why?

30 Is it easy/hard to use a dictionary?

Note that the spelling interview is an adaptation and extension of both 'The Reading Interview' (J. Harste & C. Burke, 1977) and 'The Writing Interview' (D. de Ford).

5 DICTATION OR WORD LISTS

Some children may never be willing to attempt unknown words. It is therefore impossible to use samples of their writing to analyse the strategies they are using for spelling. In such cases it may be necessary to dictate a number of sentences or individual words for children to attempt. When doing this, explain to the children that you do not expect them to be sure of the spelling of many of the words but that you want to see how they think the words are spelt. Also tell them that their work will not be marked.

Words chosen should have features which will help ascertain the children's stage of development. An example of such a list is taken from Temple, Nathan and Burris (1982):

late: Kathy was late to school again today.

wind: The wind was loud last night.

shed: The wind blew down our shed.

jumped: The frog jumped into the river.

chirped: The bird chirped when she saw a worm.

once: Jim rode his bike into a creek once.

learned: I learned to count at school.

shove: Don't shove your neighbour when you line up.

trained: I trained my dog to lie down and roll over.

year: Next year you'll have a new teacher.

shock: Electricity can shock you if you aren't careful.

stained: The ice cream spilled and stained my shirt.

chick: The egg cracked open and a chick climbed out.

drive: Jim's sister is learning how to drive.

The use of spelling tests

Norm-referenced tests, criterion-referenced tests and diagnostic tests are available for spelling. However, their usefulness is fairly limited and more detailed information may be derived from the forms of assessment already mentioned.

A norm-referenced test may be used to compare one group of children with another, but consideration should be given to both the content and sample used in the test as well as the date when the test was constructed. The norms related to such tests may be out of date and may have been obtained from population samples in other countries.

Criterion-referenced tests are designed to test whether or not particular objectives have been achieved. Consequently such tests are best devised by the classroom teacher with the class and individual objectives within the spelling programme in mind.

Diagnostic tests are used to identify specific learning problems. Such diagnosis is better achieved by analysing an individual's personal writing.

REASONS FOR NOT USING PUBLISHED FORMAL TESTS

Reasons are as follows:

- A test score provides no information about spelling strategies used.

- Two children may achieve the same test score even though they may apply entirely different strategies and have vastly different needs.

- Such tests do not measure attitudes towards spelling.

- They tend to focus on negative aspects rather than highlighting positive achievements.

- Performance on a test may not be reflected in children's writing.

- Children are usually not able to proof-read their work before spelling is assessed.

- Norms are usually based on age groups rather than stages of development.

- Such tests rarely test real spelling objectives such as the ability to form generalisations.

- They emphasise correctness rather than analysing the logic behind children's spelling attempts.

- Words tested may not be relevant to children's writing needs.

Overall, such assessment techniques do not provide a record of children's progress, and provide less information about the strategies children are using in their spelling than teacher observation and analysis of writing samples.

Evaluation

Having analysed the data gathered from a variety of assessment procedures, the class programme should be developed according to the perceived needs of the class, groups and individuals. Appropriate teaching strategies can be devised to match the stages of development of spelling evident in children's writing. Analysis of both children's achievements and errors will indicate appropriate objectives and teaching methods.

EVALUATION OF CHILDREN'S WRITING SAMPLES

EXAMPLE 1

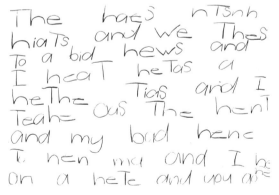

The mini bike shop and we went
to a big slide and I fell off and
my dad had to catch me . . .   *7.5 years*

Positive aspects

The child:

- demonstrates an understanding of the function of print
- shows a willingness to write and to take risks
- has the concept of a word and understands that print is written from left-to-right and top-to-bottom, that letters are used to write words and that there are spaces between words
- has a visual memory for high frequency words
- has legible handwriting
- realises that words contain a vowel
- is in between the precommunicative and semiphonetic stages.

Possible instruction

The child has no idea of the sound-symbol relationships. This could be assisted by the following:

1 Teach sound-symbol relationships in the context of other language work (see pages 22 to 23, and 28); individual assistance may be required to help this child acquire these skills.

2 Assist the child to understand that the sounds heard in a word provide an indication of the way the written word may be represented. The following technique used by Elkonin (1973) may be necessary:

- The child is given pictures of objects. Below each picture is a rectangle divided into squares according to the number of sounds in the name of the object.

- The child is given some counters. The child says the word aloud and places a counter for each sound in the corresponding square of the diagram below the picture.

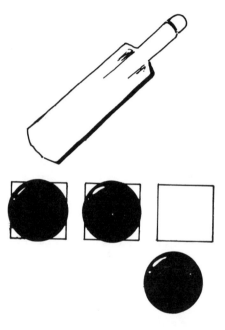

- This activity is gradually changed from an oral analysis with the use of counters and squares to a silent activity.

This procedure has also been used by Marie Clay (1979).

The teacher could also work with the child while she is writing, asking the child to state the sentence to be written and encouraging her to listen for the sounds in the words.

Be sure that the child is involved in group activities such as modelling wall stories, string writing, class diaries, etc., and is alerted to features of words in shared reading activities.

EXAMPLE 2

red Bak Spideros.
The bir of The red on
The bake of The
Spidere is The galfe
or poson. The pop is
Karont kil you put The
Big spideros can kil
kil you so when you
see one you shod kil
them.
The rrop door spidoros
is The best.
Cwry '83

6.5 years

The bit of the red on the back of the spider is the pack of poison. The babies can't kill you but the big spiders can kill you so when you see one you should kill them. The trapdoor spider is the best.

Positive aspects

The child:

- has spelt three-quarters of the words correctly
- understands the functions of print
- has knowledge of the concepts of print
- is willing to attempt unknown words
- represents all sounds heard in a word
- is moving from the phonetic to the transitional stage
- has a body of known words, mostly high frequency words
- can form generalisations (has done so with the use of a final 'e', to the point of over-generalisation).

Possible instruction

1 The child needs further opportunities for writing to allow for experimentation with 'b' and 'p'; at this stage the confusion is most likely only developmental.

2 The child is obviously aware that the spelling of 'spider' may not be correct as it is attempted in two ways. With the child's interest in spiders, it would be most appropriate to provide books on this topic in which the word 'spider' could be found. It could then be copied, learned and written into the child's personal word book. The word 'poison' may also be located in a similar way.

3 Words such as 'kill' and 'pack' and 'back' are ideal for teaching the spelling of not just an isolated word, but a group of words with the same visual pattern. For example:

kill, killing, still, fill, will, willing, thrill, killer

pack, **back**, stack, packing, crack, cracker, tack, track, tracker.

4 If you have a class word list of plural forms, refer to it to see if 'spiders' and 'babies' are on the list; if not, add them. There may be enough words on the list which end in 'y' from which the child could form a generalisation about this type of plural.

EXAMPLE 3

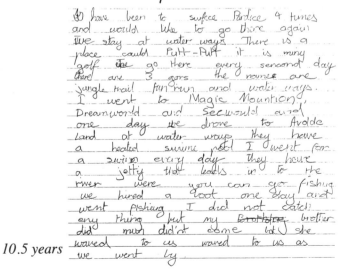

10.5 years

Positive aspects

The child:

- has spelt eight ninths of the words correctly
- is willing to attempt unknown words
- has a large body of known words
- is aware of the fact that a sound may be represented by a variety of symbols
- is aware of the use of an apostrophe in contractions (even though the use is incorrect)
- is beginning to be aware of the use of capital letters for proper nouns
- uses correct syntactic forms of verbs, and is aware that some past tenses are formed in ways other than by adding 'ed'.

Possible instruction

1 The child needs to be aware of the importance of proof-reading (writing for an audience would provide a purpose for this). The child would hopefully identify the words 'second', 'boat' and 'any'.

2 Attention should be given to highlighting the morphological relationships between words:

Dreamworld, Seaworld

sea, Seaworld

any, anything

didn't, did not.

3 Highlight compound words in word lists and reading materials. In this piece of writing note:

> everything, anything.

4 Point out words in the environment when on excursions. In this piece of writing draw attention to words such as 'Surfers Paradise', 'mini golf', 'Seaworld' and 'Magic Mountain' which would have been written in the environment. Perhaps the child could refer back to brochures or post cards from the holiday to confirm the spelling of such words.

5 Discuss the use of capital letters for names.

6 Build up verb family lists:

> swim, swimming
>
> fish, fishing.

7 Build up a word list based on the word 'mini':

> mini skirt, mini bike, mini mart, minimum, mini bus, miniature.

8 Assist with the spelling of 'where' by using the mnemonics 'here' and 'where'.

9 Encourage the child to attempt the word 'called' in other ways and to determine which one looks right. When the correct form is identified it could be related to both the meaning relationship with 'call', 'calling', 'recall', and the visual pattern relationship with words such as 'tall', 'small', 'smaller', 'fall', 'falling'.

EXAMPLE 4

13 years

Positive aspects

The child:

- has spelt two thirds of the words correctly
- is willing to attempt unknown words
- has a body of known words
- is able to copy words (e.g. 'The Reading Centre')
- can keep a visual image of a word
- is aware of sound-symbol relationships
- has concepts of print
- is aware of the function of written language and is aware of an audience
- is willing to self-correct.

Possible instruction

It is important to build up this student's self esteem, since the child would be considered a poor speller by others and is likely to have a poor self-image.

1 Point out the words which are correct, and praise all attempts at spelling words and the willingness to self-correct.

2 Assist the child to proof-read by referring to resources such as previous letters for the spelling of the words 'I', 'Dear' and 'Thursday', and by encouraging the student to read the piece aloud to note the mistakes with words such as trying (trier) and coming here (came he). If the latter words are not detected as being unsuitable, oral language needs to be developed through many opportunities for both discussion and modelling.

3 Teach the correct spelling of the high frequency words 'will' and 'like' and provide the student with a list of high frequency words (see Appendix 1) for personal reference, as these words are not likely to be displayed in a post primary school. Establish a contract with the student; for example, an agreement to learn a number of high frequency words each week. Be sure that expectations are realistic. Assist the student to learn these words by demonstrating appropriate strategies:

- learn 'here' and 'there' together
- use mnemonics:
     teach 'would' and 'could' together
     teach 'go' and 'going' together.

4 To teach the spelling of 'hardest' ask the student to attempt the spelling of 'hard'. If the student is unable to do so, write it for him to copy using the 'look, say, cover, write, check' technique.

5 Continue to encourage the writing of letters and have someone reply to them. This could be done with another supportive student who is a competent speller.

6 Provide many opportunities for writing and modelling, and encourage reading.

7 Keep dated copies of the student's writing and comment on the development of spelling strategies. Encourage the student to self-evaluate this progress.

8 Allow the student more flexibility in obtaining assistance from others before publishing writing.

9 Do not deal with too many errors from the one piece of writing.

EXAMPLE 5   And the forest is big   *18.9.84, 5.8 years*

I went to Sherbrooke forest

19.9.84

Positive aspects

The child:

- is willing to write and attempt unknown words
- is aware of the function of print
- has a known body of words
- has developed concepts of print and the ability to use space for writing
- is in the phonetic stage of development, representing all sounds in a word
- has shown development, even within one day (note the spelling of 'forest').

Possible instruction

1 Encourage the willingness to write and take risks, particularly trying to extend the quantity of writing by modelling more than one sentence and by suggesting that more than one page may be used for daily writing.

2 Add the child's known words to class and personal word lists.

3 Assist self-evaluation by pointing out the change in the spelling of 'forest'.

4 If desired, show the child how to spell 'Sherbrooke' and teach the 'look, say, cover, write, check' technique for copying.

5 Continue reading and class writing activities.

EVALUATION OF SPELLING PROGRAMME

The teacher should continually review objectives in the light of children's spelling strengths and weaknesses. Evaluating the programme can be achieved through questions such as:

1 Am I dealing with spelling in relation to writing?

2 Am I developing spellers willing to take risks, by providing positive reinforcement for each attempt?

3 Were the overall objectives that I planned at the beginning of the year appropriate? If not, what needs to be changed?

4 Am I aware of the children's self-esteem and self-image?

5 Am I doing spelling activities on a daily basis and in all curriculum areas?

6 Am I assisting children to develop beyond their initial capabilities?

7 Am I developing class word lists and making sufficient use of these?

8 Am I catering for class, group and individual needs?

9 Am I relating the activities to children's stages of development?

10 Am I providing a variety of resources for children to use?

11 Am I providing models of correct spelling through a variety of activities?

12 Have I explained to the parents the objectives of my spelling programme?

13 Does my spelling programme reflect the school policy, and do my activities reflect the objectives of my programme?

14 Are the children in my class aware of the objectives of my spelling programme?

CHILD SELF-EVALUATION

A share of the responsibility for evaluation should eventually be accepted by the child. This may be achieved through:

- periodical examinations of previous writing samples, with the child commenting on attempted spelling and the range of known words
- teacher-child discussions which highlight achievement and make decisions about future objectives
- the child proof-reading and editing her own writing prior to publication
- discussion with other children in group conferences during which achievements and problems are explored.

RECORD KEEPING

Records are kept for the teacher, child and parent to reflect on achievements and development, and for the teacher to plan future activities.

Record keeping should be easy to keep up to date and contain information that is relevant to children's progress and planning of classroom activities.

TEACHER RECORDS

1 The **yearly class programme** should state aims and objectives expected to be achieved for the ensuing year.

2 The **weekly class programme** should state short-term goals and planned activities. This may also be used as a diary, to note special achievements and aspects to be dealt with in the following week.

3 **Classroom word lists** are a record of words studied.

4 **Records of individual achievements** may be as follows:

- *Writing folder* — This could contain selected, dated examples of children's writing retained throughout the year. Significant developments in spelling could be noted on particular pieces of writing, e.g. 'First indication of over-generalisation of the silent ''e'' '.

- *Spelling checklist* — This could be attached to each child's folder. The checklist should be relevant to the stage of development and, for a beginning speller, may include the following items:
  - knows names of letters of the alphabet
  - uses conventional directionality
  - writes with spaces between words
  - uses phonetic strategy
  - is willing to attempt unknown words
  - has a known body of words
  - is interested in words.

Note that checklists for each stage of development can be devised by referring to Chapter 4 which outlines the characteristics of each stage.

- *Individual word lists or word books and 'have a go' cards* — These provide an indication of known words, interest in words and strategies for attempting unknown words.

- *Record cards* — These may be in the form of a checklist or an anecdotal record:

Checklist

Name
Attitude
Achievements

Dates
demonstrated

Anecdotal Record

Name
Date

Significant Incident

Action

- *Contracts* — These may be formed between the teacher and child, both reaching a decision about expected achievements over an ensuing period of time. These contracts should be able to be easily fulfilled within a short period of time so that the child experiences success. A sample contract follows:

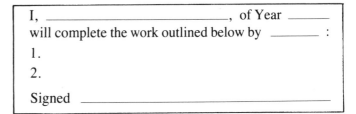

I, _____, of Year _____
will complete the work outlined below by _____ :
1.
2.
Signed _____

STUDENT RECORDS

Student records may be in the form of:

1 **Diaries or anecdotal records** in which children note any significant event in relation to their spelling.

2 **Checklists** — These examples are from the Primary English Teaching Association, 1982.

Am I Becoming a Good Speller?

- I care about spelling.
- I write often.
- I proof-read my writing.
- I read every day.
- I explore words.
- I check to be sure.
- I learn new spellings.

Am I a Good Speller?

- I am willing to attempt unknown words.
- I know how to spell some words correctly.
- I know how to use resources to check spellings.
- I know that nobody knows how to spell every word.

- I can attempt unknown words in a variety of ways.
- I proof-read for spelling errors.
- I am interested in words.

3 **Word lists, word book, 'have a go' cards** and **contracts** are also part of the children's records.

EVALUATION OF PUBLISHED SPELLING RESOURCES

No published material can in itself develop children's spelling proficiency. The strengths and weaknesses of such resources should be examined in relation to what is known about how children best learn to spell, and according to class programme objectives.

Evaluative questions may include:

- Are the activities based on what is currently known about the teaching of spelling?
- Do the activities highlight the most important features of the English orthography?
- Is there likely to be a transfer from the activities to the children's writing?
- Are the activities purposeful?
- Are the words studied words the children wish to use in their writing?
- Do the activities take into account the children's stages of development?
- Do the activities assist children to see relationships between words?
- Do the activities encourage children to form generalisations?
- Are the activities presented in an interesting way?
- Do the activities develop an interest in words?
- Are the activities really spelling activities?

Overall, it is important to note that evaluation is both the basis of all teaching and the reflection of the success of the teaching programme.

References

Am I Becoming a Good Speller?, Primary English Teaching Association, Rozelle, NSW, 1982.

Clay, M., *Reading: The Patterning of Complex Behaviour*, 2nd edn., Heineman Educational Books, New Zealand, 1979.

Elkonin, D. B., 'U.S.S.R.', in Downing, J. (ed), *Comparative Reading*, Macmillan, New York, 1973, pp. 551-580.

Temple, C. A., Nathan, R. G. & Burris, N. A., *The Beginnings of Writing*, Allyn and Bacon, Boston, 1982.

8
Considerations for English as a Second Language learners

There is little empirical evidence concerning the effects of native language on spelling in English. However, recent studies in Australia, conducted through the centre for Studies in Literacy at the University of Wollongong under the direction of Brian Cambourne, have confirmed that the sorts of strategies used by children from a non-English-speaking background are similar to those used by children from an English-speaking background.

These strategies include:

- phonemic analysis of words
- use of surrounding print
- recall of known words
- assistance from others
- repetition of particular letters and words.

However, while English-speaking children use their knowledge of oral English as a resource for spelling, non-English-speaking children are unable to do this. Consequently the non-English-speaking child may be developing the medium of oral language at the same time as that of written language.

It is important for teachers to keep in mind that non-English-speaking children cannot be expected to write what they cannot produce orally.

Nonetheless, the value of the child's native language should not be ignored. If children are literate in their first language, they already know a great deal about spelling:

'What a child knows about one expression of language can support growth and development in another . . . What the child learns about language from having read a book for example becomes available linguistic data for output in another expression of language like writing' (Harste, Burke and Woodward, 1982).

Hammond and Beecher (1984) support this in claiming:

'It appears that the concepts such children learn about what 'a language' is, how language works, and the sorts of functions that language can be used for, can be transferred from one language to another. Similarly, the sorts of concepts that children learn about writing, especially the textual features of writing, from their first language, are easily transferred to the second language'

However, even though children may be familiar with a different system, they still need a great deal of exposure to English print to enable them to work out the underlying principles of the English written code.

An example of a Vietnamese child's writing in the precommunicative stage

As Cronell (1979) states:

'If the native language uses a non-alphabetic writing system then students must learn the notion that symbols (letters) represent sounds, rather than syllables (as in Japanese) or words (as in Chinese). If the native language uses an alphabetic writing system, but not the Roman alphabet (such languages as Hindi), a new alphabet must be learned, although the notion of sound-spelling relations would not be new. If the native language uses an alphabet related to the Roman alphabet (such as Greek and Cyrillic), a number of new letters must be learned; in addition, some native-language sound-to-spelling correspondences must be unlearned; for example, in Greek P represents /r/ and in Russian H represents /n/.'

Cronell (1979) also states that 'differences in pronunciation can produce spelling errors related to these pronunciations. For example, while /r/ and /l/ can be easily spelled in Standard English, their spelling could be a problem for speakers who do not differentiate between these sounds.'

What is most important for the children to learn is the system underlying English spelling; that is, the nature of the English orthography (see Chapter 2).

They should have many opportunities to write for themselves, particularly if they have not had access to writing implements before starting school.

English as a Second Language learners require the same opportunities for formulating and hypothesis-testing about the English writing system as English-speaking children, and this should occur in an environment which totally accepts and nurtures such a learning process.

References

Cronell, B. A., 'Spelling English as a Second Language' in M. Celce-Murcia and L. McKintosh (eds), *Teaching English as a Second or Foreign Language*, Newbury House, Rowley, Mass., 1979.

Hammond, J. & Beecher, B., 'Literacy Development, Through the Process Approach to Writing, of English-as-a-Second-Language Children — A Two Year Study', paper presented at the Tenth Australian Reading Conference, Melbourne, 1984.

Harste J. C., Burke C. L. & Woodward V. A., 'Initial Encounters with Print' in Judith A. Langer & M. Trika Smith-Burke (eds), *Reader Meets Author/Bridging the Gap*, International Reading Association, Newark, Del., 1982.

Appendices

Appendix 1 — Salisbury word list

A CORE VOCABULARY FROM CHILDREN'S WRITING.
100 WORDS MOST FREQUENTLY WRITTEN
BY ADELAIDE CHILDREN

1-50

the	on	there	go
and	went	up	as
I	had	she	her
a	is	me	saw
to	then	out	came
was	for	got	him
it	said	with	back
we	when	at	after
in	so	you	are
of	that	all	about
he	but	his	very
my	one	day	
they	were	have	

Words 1-50 account for 49% of all words written.

51-100

down	what	their	Mum
be	house	around	next
home	this	if	put
like	time	who	us
some	will	found	did
them	going	night	come
would	off	see	now
not	could	little	door
because	two	people	just
into	took	do	Christmas
get	over	started	told
from	an	man	
our	by	ran	

Words 51-100 account for 10% of all words written.

Appendix 2 — Word derivations

L	**= Latin**
Gk	**= Greek**
OF	**= Old French**
ME	**= Middle English**

Gk	akrobatos — walking up high
ME	allien — to bind to
L	alter — other
L	altus — high
L	ambi — both
Gk	amphi — both
L	annus — year
Gk	anonymos — without name
L,Gk	aqua — water
Gk	artery — to raise
Gk	arthron — joint
OF	assembler — to gather
Gk	astron — star
L	atmosphaera — vapor spheres
L	audire — to hear

Gk	auto — self		L	conflictus — act of striking together
L	avis — bird		L	constituere — to set up
			L	constructus — to build
Gk	bacterion — staff		L	consumere — to take
Gk	baros — pressure		L	contra — against
L	bene — well		L	corpus — a body
L	bi, bin — two		L	credere — to believe
Gk	biblio — book		L	cultus — to cultivate
Gk	bios — life		Gk	cyclos — a wheel
Gk	botanicus — of herbs		Gk	cyl, cycl — circle
L	cap — take		L	de — down from, out of
L	censere — to assess or tax		Gk	deca — ten
L	centum — a hundred		Gk	demokratia — popular government
Gk	chroma, chromatas — colour		Gk	demos — the people
Gk	chronos — time		L	dens, dentis — tooth
L	circulus — circle		OF	departir — to depart
L	circum — around		Gk	derma — skin
Gk	cis — to cut		Gk	dialektus — to converse
ME	citizien — city		Gk	dialogos — to speak through
L	civilis — civilian		L	dico, dictum — to speak
L	clude — to shut		L	dict — to say
L	colonia — farmer		L	duc — to lead
L	companio — associate		L	duo — two
L	concilium — meeting			

Gk	elastos — flexible		Gk	gastros — belly
Gk	elektron — beaming sun		Gk	gene — birth
Gk	enthousiazein — to be inspired		L	generis — family
Fr	environ — around		L	genero — produce
Gk	epikos — work, speech, poem		Gk	geo — earth
L	equus — a horse		L	gestus — to bear
L	erodere — to eat away		L	glacies — ice
Gk	ethnos — nation, people		Gk	gramma — writing
Gk	ethos — behaviour		Gk	grapho — I write
L	evaporatus— to pass off in vapour		L	gravis — heavy
L	exaggerare — to heap up		L	gubernare — to govern, steer
L	experiri — to try		Gk	gyne, gynaecos — woman
L	exter, exterus — being on the outside, foreign			
			L	habitare — to inhabit
L	facio, factuon — make, do		Gk	haema — blood
L	fer — to bear, carry		Gk	hecton — a hundred
L	ferrum — iron		Gk	hemi — half
L	finis — end		Gk	hepta — seven
OF	flyght — flight		Gk	heteros — other
L	forma — form, shape		Gk	hexa — six
L	fortis — strong		L	hibernus — of winter
L	fugitum — flee		Gk	historia — inquiry
			Gk	homoeos — same
			Gk	huder, hydra — water
			Gk	hypnos — sleep

L   inferus — situated beneath, lower

L   instare — to stand upon

L   interrumpere — to break off

L   investigatus — to track

L   ject — to throw

L   judex — to judge

L   jungere — to join

Gk   keramikos — pottery

Gk   kilo — one thousand

Gk   kline — bed

Gk   kolossos — giant statue

Gk   komoidia — to revel and sing

Gk   kosmos — universe

Gk   kykloma — wheel

L   latus — side

L   lectus — to read

L   liber — free

L   lingua — language

L   litterae — letters, literature

Gk   logos — word

Gk   logy — speaking about an area of study

L   luna — moon

L   lustrare — to light up

L   macro, Gk. macros — large, long

L   magnus — large

L   major — greater

L   mal — bad

L   manus — the hand

L   mare — sea

L   mater — a mother

L   maximus — greatest

L   medius — middle

Gk   mega — large

L   mens — mind

Gk   meta — after, change of

Gk   metron — a measure

Gk   metropolis — mother city

L   metrum — measure

Gk   micros — small

L   mille — one thousand

L   minimus — smallest

Gk   mimis — to mimic, copy

L   mitto — I send

L   moles — mass

Gk   mon, monos — one

L   multis — many

L	murus — wall	
L	natio — race	
Gk	nautes — sailor, traveller	
Gk	neuron — nerve	
L	nomen — name	
L	novem — nine	
L	novus — new	
L	nox — night	
L	nullus — nothing, none	
L	nuncio — to speak out	
L	nux — kernel, nut	
Gk	okto — eight	
L	omnis — all	
Gk	opthalmos — eye	
Gk	opticos — sight	
L	opus — work	
L	ordos — order	
Gk	orthos — correct, straight, normal	

Gk	pan — all
L	par — equal
Gk	para — alongside, against
L	pars, partis — a part
L	particula — part
Gk	pathy — feeling
L	ped — foot
L	pel, pell, puls — drive
L	pend — weigh, hang
Gk	penta — five
Gk	peri — around
L	pet — seek
Gk	philo — I love
Gk	phobos — fear
Gk	phono — sound
Gk	photos — light
L	plico — to fold/involve
L	plor — weep aloud
Gk	pneuma — air
Gk	polis — city, state
Gk	politikos — political
L	pollutionem — to soil
Gk	polys — many
L	populus — people
L	porto — carry

L	praemium — booty, profit, reward		L	septem — seven
L	prehendo — to grasp		L	servo — I keep
L	press — to press		L	similus — like, similar
L	primitivus — first or eldest of its kind		L	sist — to start from
L	proprius — own		L	sol — the sun
L	prospectus — view		L	solutus — to loosen, to solve
L	proximare — to come near		L	solvo — I solve
Gk	psyche — the mind		Gk	sophia — wisdom
Gk	pyr — fire		L	specere — to look at
			L	spect — to look at
L	qualis — of what type?		L	spirare — to breathe
L	quantis — of what amount?		L	spire — to breathe into
			Gk	statos — placed or standing
L	radius — a spoke		L	status — to stand
L	repraesentare — to represent		L	stella — a star
L	respublica — commonwealth, civil affairs		Gk	straphe — a turning
L	rodere — to gnaw		L	stratus — spread out
			L	structum — to build
L	sacer, sacrum — holy		L	sumo — I take
Gk	sauros — lizard		L	superus — upper
L	scribe — to write		Gk	sym — together
L	sculpere — to carve		Gk	syn — together
Gk	sema — signal, sign			
L	senatus — council of elders			
L	sent — to feel			

L	tango — touch		L	vivo — live
Gk	tapes — rug, carpet		L	voc or vok — voice
Gk	taxis — an arrangement		L	volv — to turn/roll
Gk	techne — art, skill		L	vovo — call
Gk	tele — distant		L	Vulcanus (god Vulcan) — volcano
L	temperatura — mixture			
L	terra — earth		ME	weven — to weave
L	tertius — a third			
Fr	textere — to weave		Gk	zoon — living thing
L	textilis — woven			
L	textura — texture			
Gk	theoria — a sight, view			
Gk	theos — god			
Gk	thermos — hot			
Gk	topos — position, place			
L	totus — entire			
L	tyrannus — tyrant			
L	unus — one			
L	vacuus — empty			
L	venio — to come			
L	vert — to turn			
L	videre — to see			
L	vinco, victum — I conquer, to conquer			

Appendix 3 — Prefixes

a — not, without

ab — away from

ad — to, toward, against

ante — before

anti — against, opposite

arch — chief, senior

at — to, toward

auto — self

bi — two

circum — around

co — together

con — with, together

contra — against

counter — in opposition, against

de — down, away from

dia — through, across

dis — away, not, the reverse of

dys — bad, badly

en — to cause, provide

epi — to, against, added on

ex — out of, away from

exo — outside

extra — outside

fore — previously, in front of

hyper — extra, over, beyond

hypo — under, below

in — not

in, im — within, toward

infra — below, underneath

inter — between

intra — inside of

mal — bad, badly

micro — small

mini — small

mis — wrongly, badly

mono — single

multi — many

non — against, not

ob — in the way of

omni — all, general

pan — whole

para — alongside, similar to

per — through, thorough

poly — many

post — after

pre — before

pro — in favour of

proto — earliest, original

pseudo — pretended

quad — four

re — back, again

retro — backwards

semi — half

sub — under, less than

super — over, more than

supra — above, beyond

trans — across, through

tri — three

ultra — beyond

un — not, the reverse of

uni — single, one

vice — in place of

Appendix 4 — Suffixes

THOSE WHICH OFTEN INDICATE THAT THE WORD IS A NOUN:

-age

-al

-ance

-ant

-ate

-ee — names of people to whom something is done

-ence

-ent

-er, -or, -ar — people or things that do certain work

-ese — indicating persons from a particular country

-ess — female form

-hood — state of being

-ice

-ician

-ism

-ist — often denotes an occupation

-ment

-ness — state of being

-sion

-tain

-tion

-ure

THOSE WHICH INDICATE THE ADJECTIVAL FORM OF A WORD

-able

-al

-er

-est

-ette, let

-ful

-fully

-ible

-ic

-ical

-ish

-ive

-less

-ous

-proof

-some

-worthy

THOSE WHICH INDICATE THE VERBAL FORM

-ate

-ed

-en

-ing

-ise, -ize, -yze

THOSE WHICH INDICATE THE ADVERBIAL FORM

-ly

-wards

-ways

-wide

-wise

Appendix 5 — Sound/symbol groupings

compiled by Marilyn Woolley

MELBOURNE STATE COLLEGE   CURRICULUM STUDIES DEPARTMENT   PHONEME-GRAPHEME GROUPINGS

Below is a list of some of the phoneme-grapheme groupings and patterns in English. This list may be used as a reminder of the variety of ways that a sound may be represented.

a	pat	u	pup	i	pit	e	pet	o	pot
ai	plait	o	front	y	funny	ie	friend	oh	Johnson
i	meringue	oe	does	ey	honey	ea	lead	ho	honour
		ou	tough	ie	sieve	ai	said	a	was
		oo	blood	u	busy	u	bury	ow	knowledge
		a	usable	a	village	a	any	ou	cough
				o	women	ue	guess	au	because
				ia	marriage	ei	leisure		
				e	pretty				
				ai	captain				
				ei	forfeit				
				ui	build				

a	cage	u	education	I	I	o	photo	e	these
ay	day	eau	beauty	y	type	oe	hoe	i	ski, naive
ey	prey	eu	Europe	i	ripe	ow	yellow	ee	feet
eigh	weigh	ew	ewe	igh	sigh	owe	owes	ei	ceiling
aigh	straight	you	youth	ie	lie	oa	loaf	ie	believe
ei	reign			eye	eyes	oh	oh	ea	tea
ai	train			eigh	height	ew	sew	i	machine
ea	great			is	isle	eau	beau	eo	people
et	bouquet			ais	aisle	ough	though	oe	amoeba
au	gauge			ig	sign	au	chauvinist	ay	quay
				a	naive			is	chassis
				ai	Shanghai			ey	key
								ae	archaeology

ow	cow	a	last	aw	paw	o	who	ere	there
hou	hour	ar	garden	augh	taught	oo	room	eir	their
ou	house	aa	bazaar	our	four	wo	two	are	mare
ough	bough	ear	heart	or	for	oe	shoe	air	pair
		au	laugh	ore	more	ough	through	eir	heir
		er	sergeant	oor	floor	ou	group	ayor	mayor
		ah	galah	au	exhaust	ue	true	ear	tear
		al	half	oar	board	u	Honolulu		
		are	are	al	talk	ui	fruit		
		uar	guard	a	call	ew	jewel		
				orps	corps				
				ar	wharf				

ear	p<u>ear</u>l	oo	b<u>oo</u>k	ere	h<u>ere</u>	oi	<u>oi</u>l	or	doct<u>or</u>
ir	thi<u>r</u>ty	ou	w<u>ou</u>ld	ear	f<u>ear</u>	oy	b<u>oy</u>	er	moth<u>er</u>
er	f<u>er</u>n	u	p<u>u</u>sh	eer	b<u>eer</u>	uoy	b<u>uoy</u>	yr	mart<u>yr</u>
ur	t<u>ur</u>n			eir	w<u>eir</u>d				
or	w<u>or</u>ld			eor	th<u>eor</u>y				
olo	c<u>olo</u>nel								

p	<u>p</u>at	t	<u>t</u>op	s	<u>is</u>	s	<u>us</u>	m	<u>m</u>e
pp	pe<u>pp</u>er	tt	li<u>tt</u>le	ss	po<u>ss</u>ess	ss	a<u>ss</u>ist	mm	co<u>mm</u>on
pe	pi<u>pe</u>	te	la<u>te</u>	se	ho<u>se</u>	se	promi<u>se</u>	me	ti<u>me</u>
		ed	finish<u>ed</u>	si	bu<u>si</u>ness	c	con<u>c</u>eit	mb	co<u>mb</u>
		cht	ya<u>cht</u>	es	cloth<u>es</u>	ce	la<u>ce</u>	gm	diaphra<u>gm</u>
		ct	indi<u>ct</u>	x	<u>x</u>ylophone	sw	<u>sw</u>ord	mn	hy<u>mn</u>
		pt	recei<u>pt</u>	z	<u>z</u>ebra	st	li<u>st</u>en	lm	ca<u>lm</u>
		tte	cigare<u>tte</u>	zz	bu<u>zz</u>	sc	<u>sc</u>ythe		
		th	<u>th</u>yme			ps	<u>ps</u>alm		
		bt	dou<u>bt</u>			sth	a<u>sth</u>ma		

n	<u>on</u>	f	<u>if</u>	d	sai<u>d</u>	l	<u>l</u>et	th	<u>th</u>is
nn	i<u>nn</u>	ff	o<u>ff</u>	dd	mu<u>dd</u>y	ll	ca<u>ll</u>ing	the	ba<u>the</u>
ne	la<u>ne</u>	fe	li<u>fe</u>	de	spa<u>de</u>	le	pi<u>le</u>		
kn	<u>kn</u>ow	ph	<u>ph</u>otograph	ed	roll<u>ed</u>				
dne	We<u>dne</u>sday	lf	ha<u>lf</u>	ld	wou<u>ld</u>				
pn	<u>pn</u>eumonia	gh	trou<u>gh</u>						
gn	<u>gn</u>at	u	lie<u>u</u>tenant						

w	wet	k	kite	r	rabbit	b	bit	h	he
wh	when	kk	trekked	r	terror	bb	ribbon	wh	who
o	once	k	like	re	more	be	robe		
ui	suite	ck	duck	rre	bizarre				
u	language	ch	chorus	wr	write				
		c	cat	rh	rhythm				
		che	ache	rt	mortage				
		lk	talk						
		qu	quay						
		que	antique						
g	go	sh	shop	ch	chicken	j	jug	x	fox
gg	lagged	t	nation	te	righteous	g	giant	xe	axe
gh	ghost	s	sugar	c	cello	d	soldier	cks	lacks
gue	fatigue	ce	ocean	t	creature	dge	judge		
		ss	tissue			ag	cage	qu	queen
		sc	conscience					ch	choir
		ch	chalet					y	yellow
		si	fusion					u	use
		chs	fuchsia						
e	the	or	doctor						
u	industy	er	writer						
i	medicine	a	about						

Appendix 6 — Dictionaries and word books

This list does not include the normal range of dictionaries and thesauri normally purchased for primary and elementary schools.

Doubleday Children's Picture Dictionary, Doubleday, New York, 1986.

Espy, W. R., *A Children's Almanac of Words at Play*, Potter, New York, 1982.

Roget's Student Thesaurus, Harper Collins, New York, 1991.

Thorndike Barnhart Student Dictionary, Harper Collins, New York, 1993.

Webster's New World Children's Dictionary, Prentice Hall, New York, 1991.